The
QUESTIONS
and
ANSWERS
on
DISABILITY
INSURANCE

WORKBOOK

A STEP-BY-STEP GUIDE TO SIMPLE ANSWERS

FOR YOUR COMPLEX QUESTIONS

TONY STEUER, CLU, LA, CPFFE
and MAXWELL SCHMITZ

LIFE INSURANCE SAGE PRESS

This publication is designed to provide accurate and authoritative information in regard to the subject matter covered. It is sold with the understanding that the publisher and author are not engaged in rendering legal, accounting, or other professional services. If legal advice or other expert assistance is required, the services of a competent professional should be sought.

Published by Life Insurance Sage Press
Alameda, CA

Design and composition by Greenleaf Book Group LLC
Cover design by Greenleaf Book Group LLC

Publisher's Cataloging-In-Publication Data
(Prepared by The Donohue Group, Inc.)

Steuer, Anthony.

   The questions and answers on disability insurance workbook : a step-by-step guide to simple answers for your complex questions / Tony Steuer. — 1st ed.

   p. : ill., charts ; cm.

   A companion to Questions and answers on life insurance. 2010.
   ISBN: 978-0-9845081-4-3

   1. Disability insurance—United States—Handbooks, manuals, etc. 2. Disability insurance—Law and legislation—United States—Handbooks, manuals, etc. I. Steuer, Anthony. Questions and answers on life insurance. II. Title.

HD7105.25.U6 S74 2012
368.382/00973   2012932703

Printed in the United States of America on acid-free paper

12 13 14 15 16   10 9 8 7 6 5 4 3 2 1

First Edition

CONTENTS

INTRODUCTION

Did you know that . . .

- 3 in 10 workers entering the workforce today will become disabled for some period of time before they retire (Social Security Administration, Fact Sheet, January 31, 2007)?

- more than 90 percent of disabling accidents and illnesses are not work related, which means they aren't covered by worker's compensation insurance (National Safety Council, Injury Facts, 2004)?

- most Americans don't have enough savings to meet short-term emergencies (2004 National Investment Watch Survey)?

- disability was behind nearly 50 percent of all mortgage foreclosures (*Health Affairs*, the Policy Journal of the Health Sphere, February 2, 2005)?

- 56 percent of workers who currently receive Social Security disability benefits are under age 55 (Social Security Administration, 2007 Annual Statistical Report)?

- nearly 60 percent of workers have not discussed with their families how they would handle or manage an income-limiting disability (Council on Disability Awareness, 2007 Disability Awareness Survey)?

If you're like most people, you probably found these statistics surprising. Most of us tend to think about auto insurance, homeowner's insurance, and even life insurance. Yet, dollar for dollar, long-term disability insurance may be one of the most important financial planning and protection resources available to you. Consider the following odds for any single year:

- 1 out of 8.63 that you will die during your working years, ages 18 to 65 (Social Security Administration, Period Life Table, 2007)

- 1 out of about 1,250 that you will lose your house to a fire, according to various industry sources

- 1 out of 55 that you will have an automobile accident that results in property damage, injuries, or fatalities, according to the National Highway Traffic Safety Administration ("Traffic Safety Facts 2009")

- 1 in 3 (approximately) that you will become disabled at some point during your working life.

We protect our other assets, but we often neglect to protect our most important asset: our income.

Ironically, as the preceding statistics reveal, most of us are spending money to protect ourselves and our possessions against events that are less likely to occur. The payouts for those other forms of insurance pale in comparison to the potential payouts—and, more important, the financial protection—of disability insurance. Just look at these calculations: For car insurance, the average payout is approximately $28,000 (*Motor Trend*, April 30, 2003). For life insurance, it's $257,200 (U.S. Census Bureau, March 24, 2004). But for disability insurance, the projected payout for a 35-year-old who earns $50,000 a year and is disabled for the rest of his or her life with an eligible benefit of 60 percent would have an annual benefit of $30,000 for a total payout of $900,000 (until retirement age of 65)!

Despite all of these statistics, and despite the severe potential financial impact of a disabling illness or injury, men and women often overlook the purchase of long-term disability insurance (sometimes called disability income insurance) in their financial planning. The goal of this workbook is to help you protect yourself against potential loss of income and to make sure that you can meet your cash flow needs in the event of a disability.

Disability insurance, therefore, may be one of the most important purchases you will ever make. As is the case with any important purchase, it pays to avoid the pitfalls into which you can so easily fall. The human mind seeks simple answers, but very often the simple answer is not the right answer. Proper selection of a disability insurance product requires more than simply choosing the lowest-priced policy (although sometimes that is the right choice). Many other factors must be considered in making the best choice for your situation.

For most people, consulting a qualified and objective disability insurance specialist is the best way to ensure that an appropriate decision is made given their particular set of circumstances. The problem, however, from a consumer perspective, is making sure that the advice given is professionally objective. And oftentimes the disability insurance salesperson does not service or review the disability insurance coverage. This can lead to some unwanted results for the client, such as being underinsured or not having appropriate riders (i.e., policy features).

In part I of this workbook, we will help you examine the odds of becoming disabled and how long an average disability lasts so that you better understand your risks. We will then help you calculate the impact of a disability on your finances and identify factors that affect your need for disability insurance. In part II, we'll explore how to find a good agent and a good insurance company; help you find the most affordable policy to meet your specific needs; and walk you through the process of applying for and purchasing a policy. Finally, in part III, we'll educate you about how to monitor your policy to make sure you're getting the maximum coverage you need. And, in the event that you do need to file a claim, we've provided a section that will help you learn about that process. We've also included a section about specific types of policies for businesses.

If you have an existing policy, you can use this workbook to see how your policy measures up to your current needs. And if you don't have a policy, you can use this workbook to make the best decisions possible for your needs.

Because the more informed you are, the better the choices you will make.

DISABILITY INSURANCE DECISION CHART

Part I	Part II	Part III

Evaluate Your Needs and Situation	*Evaluate Agents and Companies and Purchase a Policy*	*Understand, Maintain, and Monitor Your Policy or Make a Claim*

Step 1:
What is my current need for disability insurance?

Step 5:
Which agent or advisor can help me get the best policy for the best price?

Step 8:
Is my policy up-to-date and meeting my needs?

Step 2:
How much income protection do I need, and how much do I already have?

Step 6:
Which insurance companies should I consider working with, based on financial stability?

Step 9:
What do I need to consider before I file a claim?

Step 3:
What disability insurance policy definitions, parameters, or riders are most important to me?

Step 7:
What final points do I need to consider before completing the application process and purchasing a policy?

Step 4:
What factors in my life might affect my eligibility or my rates?

PART I

EVALUATE YOUR NEEDS AND SITUATION

STEP 1

Determine Your Need for Disability Insurance

Disability insurance seems easy to understand on the surface: You pay a premium, and if you become disabled, the insurance company replaces your income. Under the surface, however, lie important nuances that can affect your decisions. These nuances aren't daunting, though; disability insurance is like anything else: If you take the time to learn about it, you'll be able to understand it and make smart choices about what to buy.

It may surprise you, but the best place to start is *not* with a discussion of long-term disability insurance options. Instead, let's begin with a close look at your own risks and needs. And that self-education should always begin with an assessment of reality: What are your personal reasons for needing income protection? What are your chances or risks of becoming disabled? What other factors should you consider?

Answer the questions within this step the best you can, but don't worry about getting everything absolutely, inflexibly "right." This exercise isn't about perfection—no one can know the future. It's about taking a best guess. It's about considering where you are now and how you want to be protected.

(1) EXPLORING WHY YOU NEED LONG-TERM DISABILITY INSURANCE

Following are a number of scenarios or life situations that illustrate a need for long-term disability insurance. Put a check next to the descriptions below that best correspond to your needs.

I'm a primary breadwinner for my family. I have young children and *my family is absolutely dependent on my income.* If I were to become disabled tomorrow, they'd be in big trouble.

I've got debt. I have a mortgage (or mortgages), a car loan (or loans), credit cards, student loans, or some other form of *large, significant debt that I couldn't carry or burden my family or cosigners with if I became disabled* tomorrow. It would break them.

○ I don't want to burden my family with the need to take care of me, or I don't have any close family whom I could rely on to take care of me if I weren't able to earn income for myself.

○ I don't have a rainy day fund set aside to cover not only regular expenses but also potential additional expenses (medical expenses, special care) if I had to go even six months without income.

○ I don't have extensive assets that I could rely on to support my, and my family's, standard of living if I were to become disabled for some extended period of time.

Which of these scenarios best describe your situation will largely depend on what assets you have or can reasonably expect to have in the near future, what stage of life you're in, and your personal family situation. Although these aren't even all the reasons for having disability insurance, they do capture the most common motivations or reasons for purchasing it.

Becoming disabled can have not only long-term physical effects but also long-term social and psychological effects on your life beyond the financial ones. Consequently, it's important to consider your most personal reasons for considering disability insurance. The following issues are worth considering, as they can have an indirect impact on your financial situation during a disability:

- **Returning to work**: While returning to work is always a goal after incurring a disability, there is no guarantee that your work will be the same or that your compensation will be the same. You may also be able to return to work on a part-time basis only, which can cause a continued reduced income. And, depending on the disability, the medical costs you incur may be quite high because of your deductibles, co-payments, etc., even if you have medical insurance. When an employer is large enough to cover you under the Family Medical Leave Act, they are obligated to keep disabled individuals' prior positions (or comparable ones) available to them for the first twelve weeks of absence. After twelve weeks, that prior position may be filled, and the disabled person may need to apply for other jobs within the same firm or seek employment with other companies, possibly in other geographic locations.

- **Impact on family caregivers**: Disabilities often require family members, particularly spouses, to provide special care and assistance to the disabled person. This can be challenging if the resources aren't available to get help for the caregivers who themselves are working outside the home.

- **Increased risk of divorce**: Financial stress is a leading cause of divorce among adults in the United States. This is further compounded by the emotional and mental stress that often accompanies a disability. The U.S. Government's National Health Interview Survey of almost 50,000 households in 1994 showed that the proportion of disabled adults who were divorced or separated was almost 60 percent higher than the proportion for nondisabled adults. It's risky to count on your spouse's income to support you if you become disabled.

Use the space below to write down other reasons why you might consider purchasing disability insurance. Or use the space to record your thoughts on how the scenarios you selected above apply specifically to your own situation. What are your biggest concerns related to the possibility of becoming disabled?

---

2 UNDERSTANDING YOUR RISKS

Many of us tend to think of becoming disabled as something that happens to other people, particularly to those with physically demanding jobs. But as we pointed out in the introduction, only about 10 percent of all disabling injuries happen on the job. If you are young and fit, you might believe your chances of becoming disabled are less than an older person's, but statistics show that isn't the case, because you have more years during which you might become disabled. The following table makes that clear-cut point. Use the closest age to your own to determine your chances of becoming disabled and write the number down in the space provided:

Chance of becoming disabled based on age: _____

YOUR CHANCES OF BECOMING DISABLED FOR MORE THAN 90 DAYS BEFORE THE AGE OF 65		
AGE	PERCENTAGE DISABLED	ODDS OF BECOMING DISABLED
25	52%	1 out of 2
30	51%	1 out of 2
35	48%	4 out of 9
40	45%	4 out of 9
45	40%	2 out of 5
50	34%	1 out of 3
55	16%	1 out of 6

Source: 1985 Commissioner's Disability Table

Now, if you're older, this table might make you think the risks associated with becoming disabled are less than they are for a younger person. But again, that isn't the case. The problem older people face is that their disabilities tend to last much longer. And, given the fact that the age for the onset of receiving Social Security benefits has continued to rise over the years, depending on that government resource is dangerous. Although the preceding table only goes up to age 55, the retirement age for Social Security purposes will soon reach 70 years of age.

In the following table, find your age range and then read across to understand how long a disability is likely to last and the probability of a long-term disability (defined as more than three months in duration) lasting longer than five years. Fill in the appropriate information on the spaces provided below. Potential average length of a disability based on your age: _____

Probability of a long-term disability lasting five years or longer: _____

THE OLDER YOU GET, THE HIGHER YOUR CHANCES OF BEING DISABLED FOR LONGER PERIODS OF TIME		
AGE	AVERAGE LENGTH OF YOUR DISABILITY*	YOUR PROBABILITY OF DISABILITY* LASTING 5 YEARS OR MORE
20–24	69 months	30%
25–29	74 months	32%
30–34	78 months	35%
35–39	82 months	38%
40–44	85 months	40%
45–49	86 months	43%
50–54	86 months	45%
55+	84 months	46%

* For disabilities lasting three months or longer. Source: Council for Disability Awareness

Now that you understand your risk factors a bit more, let's explore your more personal motivations for purchasing a disability insurance policy.

3   WHAT'S YOUR PERSONAL DISABILITY QUOTIENT?

With a better understanding of your personal motivating factors, you can now move on to a somewhat statistical assessment of your need for life insurance based on your risk factors. You can calculate your own personal disability quotient (PDQ)—your own chance of being injured or becoming ill—that could force you to miss work for an extended period of time. You can also calculate your PDQ through an online calculator at www.whatsmypdq.org (sponsored by the Council for Disability Awareness).

1. Age/Gender

What is your age?   points   your points:_____

	male	female
<25	18	22
25–34	13	16
35–44	9	10
45–54	1	1
55+	0	0

2. Occupation

What kind of work do you do?   points   your points:_____

	points
Mostly office work/indoors	0
Little office work/indoors	8
Little physical work/outdoors	18
Mostly physical work/outdoors	20

3. Body Mass Index

Do you consider yourself to be . . .   points   your points:_____

	points
About the right size	0
Underweight	0
Overweight	8
Obese	21

4. Tobacco

Have you used tobacco products in the past year?

                                points   your points:_____

	points
Yes	10
No	0

5. Lifestyle

How healthy is your lifestyle? Consider regular physical exams, regular exercise, stress, sleep and eating habits, drug or alcohol abuse.

                                points   your points:_____

	points
Very healthy	0
About average	3
Not very healthy	7

6. Medical Conditions

Do you have or are you undergoing treatment for: diabetes, high blood pressure, high cholesterol, heart disease, cancer, chronic back or joint pain, drug, alcohol, or food addiction, anxiety or depression?

                                points   your points:_____

	points
No	0
Yes	12

Your Total Points

What do your numbers for questions one through six add up to? _____

Check the box that reflects your total points below. Read across to see your estimated chance of becoming disabled and unable to work for three months or longer before the age of 65.

	less than 25 points	5–25% chance
○	less than 25 points	5–25% chance
○	25–35 points	25–35% chance
○	36–49 points	35–50% chance
○	50+ points	50% or more chance

Provided courtesy of the Council on Disability Awareness (www.disabilitycanhappen.org)

✎ *Notes*

Your PDQ is a valuable score to have in hand. Pairing that score with your personal factors can help you develop a keen sense for your personal need for disability insurance. However, it is very IMPORTANT to keep in mind that even if your PDQ score is low, you should still consider disability insurance. Why? Because even if you are healthy right now and have low risk factors, any one of a number of medical conditions could crop up and keep you from working. Consider the following chart, which shows the many leading medical causes of long-term disabilities and what percentages of disabilities are attributed to each.

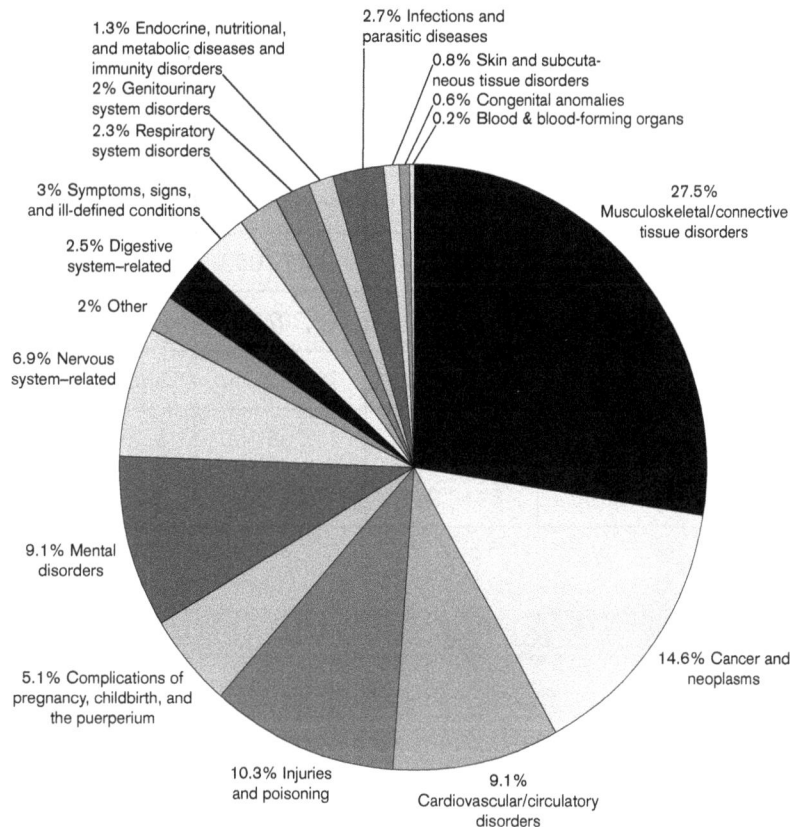

Percent of new long-term disability claims approved in the survey year. Source: The 2011 CDA Long-Term Disability Claim Review

A NOTE ON COMPREHENSIVE VS. SPECIALIZED POLICIES

Since illnesses and injuries are so unpredictable, many financial professionals recommend first purchasing comprehensive disability insurance and then, if desired, purchasing more specialized insurance policies to pay additional expenses that may come with specific illnesses (these types of policies are available). The preceding pie chart illustrates why it's important to have comprehensive coverage that protects against many common conditions.

Recall from the introduction that disability insurance (sometimes called disability income insurance) is just as important—if not more so—as car insurance, homeowner's insurance, and life insurance. Even if your chances of becoming disabled are low and you don't have strong personal motivations for protecting your income, you should consider the sheer size of the asset you would be protecting. Your potential lifetime earnings are a massive asset; they're much greater than the value of your home, for instance. And the potential size of that asset only grows as the retirement age increases.

To help you understand the importance of protecting your income, we've provided the Asset Insurance Worksheet that follows. To calculate your potential earnings, use the age and income closest to your current age and income and find your potential earnings in the table provided. You'll soon see that good health is priceless.

POTENTIAL EARNINGS TO AGE 65 IN DOLLARS (WITH 5% ANNUAL SALARY INCREASES)						
	CURRENT ANNUAL INCOME					
Age	25K	50K	75K	100K	150K	200K
30	$2,258,0005	$4,516,000	$6,774,000	$9,032,000	$13,548,000	$18,064,000
35	$1,661,000	$3,322,000	$4,983,000	$6,644,000	$9,966,000	$13,288,000
40	$1,193,000	$2,386,000	$3,580,000	$4,773,000	$7,159,000	$9,545,000
45	$827,000	$1,653,000	$2,480,000	$3,307,000	$4,960,000	$6,613,000
50	$539,000	$1,079,000	$1,618,000	$2,158,000	$3,237,000	$4,316,000
55	$314,000	$629,000	$943,000	$1,258,000	$1,887,000	$2,516,000
60	$138,000	$276,000	$414,000	$553,000	$829,000	$1,105,000

ASSET INSURANCE WORKSHEET

Asset Values

Health	Priceless
Car	$_____
Home	$_____
Potential earnings	$_____
Annual insurance premiums	$_____
Health insurance	$_____
Auto insurance	$_____
Homeowner's insurance	$_____
Income protection (disability) insurance	$_____

How do your premiums match up to the values of your assets? Are you paying the most for health insurance? How much are you paying to protect your income or potential earnings? Income protection should be something you are willing to pay a premium for, but if you're like the majority of Americans, you don't.

In the introduction, we told you that the chances of being in a serious auto accident were 1 out of 55; the chances of losing your home to a fire were about 1 out of 1,250; the chances of becoming disabled are 1 out of 3; and at the risk of becoming morbid, the chances of having health complications are 1 out of 1. Your #1 ranked asset—health—is bound to deteriorate.

The trouble is that no one believes they will personally be afflicted by a disability, and so they don't protect their potential earnings. But consider this: If you lost your home and all of your belongings and didn't have insurance, yet still had your income, you could eventually rebuild those assets. But if you lost your income and had no insurance, it's highly possible you could lose your home and have no resources to maintain your standard of living over time.

The statistics are real. You might not need a deluxe disability insurance policy, but you *do* need to have some sort of plan in place.

. . . .

You now have a solid understanding of your motivations and reasons for potentially purchasing disability insurance. It's time to explore what kinds of income protection you already have and to balance that information with your need for protection.

Note: We encourage business owners, executives, and human resources personnel to refer to the appendix, "Disability Insurance Solutions for Your Business," for a discussion about options for disability insurance protection for their employees.

DETERMINE HOW MUCH INCOME PROTECTION YOU NEED AND WHAT YOU MAY ALREADY HAVE

Since the decision to purchase disability insurance relies primarily on your needs and circumstances, it's time to turn our attention to your current financial circumstances and the benefits that may already be available to you. This assessment, while it can be a bit tough, is critically important to determining how much insurance you may need and what kind of a policy you may want to purchase. Although a number of resources, such as Social Security, are available to people who become disabled, it isn't always safe to rely on those resources alone.

In this step, we will first determine roughly how much income protection you may need. Then, to help you understand exactly how much and what type of personal disability insurance you may want to purchase, we will explore various resources that may or may not offer that protection. Finally, we will assess any current protection you may already have and compare it to your current needs.

A note before we begin: In this workbook, we focus on long-term disability insurance, although we do also talk about integrating it with other types of disability insurance. Short-term disability insurance usually covers disabilities that last fewer than 90 days, but generally, individuals cannot purchase short-term disability coverage. Typically, you will only have it as group coverage through your employer or possibly through another organization. However, considering whether or not you have short-term disability coverage is an important part of the planning process because it will be important to consider how much of your savings you might have to use before your long-term disability insurance kicks in.

(1) DETERMINING HOW MUCH INCOME PROTECTION YOU ACTUALLY NEED

Every advisor, financial columnist, and relative has a formula they think is best for determining how much long-term disability insurance you need. Some of these formulas are simple, whereas others look like something only a Wall Street numbers whiz could cook up. But don't let complexity overwhelm or discourage you. If your needs are more complex, a qualified disability insurance agent or financial advisor can help you determine the right amount for you. (We'll look at how you can find a great advisor in step 5.) For most people, however, the simplest method is the best.

To calculate how much coverage you might need, you can complete the following worksheet by listing your current monthly expenses and continued sources of income in the event of a disability. Then you can look at potential extra expenses and additional assets to help you understand what other financial burdens you may have in the future that you may need to protect yourself against. Keep in mind that these numbers do not need to be exact; they will vary based on your future circumstances. As you think about how much income you might need if you become disabled, consider how long disabilities tend to last (see pages 10) and that disability often brings additional expenses you may not currently have, such as those for COBRA medical premiums, aides, etc. We've accounted for some of these possibilities in the items in the worksheet.

THE INCREASED COSTS OF DISABILITY

Although it isn't pleasant to consider, some disabilities come with additional expenses that can be quite large. For instance, if you were unable to walk and were forced to use a wheelchair, your home might need to be renovated to be wheelchair accessible. Or you might need to purchase a new vehicle or a vehicle with special elements to meet your needs. Or you might need the use of special medical equipment that is only partially covered by your medical insurance. To give you some perspective, according to a 2005 Harvard study, better than half of all personal bankruptcies and foreclosures result from the expenses that result from a disability. While it is impossible to say what additional expenses you might face, you should consider the issue as you think about your future income needs and insurance. This is especially true if you have minimal savings that you could rely on to help cover these costs.

1. Monthly/annual income needed.

How much monthly income would you and/or your family need if you became disabled tomorrow? Let's start with your current monthly expenses. If you don't monitor these numbers closely already, take this opportunity to get to know them.

Homeowner's expenses/rent (including property taxes, insurance, dues, etc.): $_____

Car payment(s), maintenance, and insurance: $_____

Groceries: $_____

Utility bills (phone, gas, electric, cable, water, etc.): $_____

Clothing: $_____

Transportation: $_____

Child care (daycare, nanny, after-school care, etc.): $_____

Debt payments (credit cards, student loans, other outstanding debts): $_____

Medical/dental expenses and insurance premiums: $_____

Note: Keep in mind that if you become disabled and aren't working, and your family depends on your job for medical insurance coverage, your premiums could drastically increase. If you don't have other sources of medical insurance (for instance, a spouse's job/company), then do a little research to determine what personal medical coverage might cost you per month. You might ask the benefits administrator at work what it would cost you to continue your coverage with the company even if you weren't employed there (through COBRA policies) and then add 15 percent to be conservative.

Other insurance premiums (life insurance, long-term care insurance, disability insurance): $_____

Retirement funding (IRA contributions, etc.): $_____

Education expenses (current cost of private school, college, special instruction, etc.): $_____

Savings for children's college education: $_____

Note: If you were to become disabled, you wouldn't be able to rely on your income to help you cover the costs of college when your children are actually there, so you may need to plan on saving more now if helping your children pay for college is important to you.

Other savings: $_____

Travel/Entertainment: $_____

Everything else: $_____

Total Income Needed: $_____

2. Monthly income that would continue even if you were disabled.

For any item below that is typically paid out annually, divide the total by twelve to get an average monthly calculation.

Spouse or partner's salary: $_____

Current average interest and dividend income from savings and investments: $_____

Current income from a business that could continue to operate without you: $_____

Rental property income: $_____

Current Social Security benefits, disability benefits, or other similar benefits: $_____

Regular monetary gifts from family: $_____

Other passive income: $_____

Total Passive Income: $_____

3. Gap between monthly expenses and monthly income in the event of a total disability.

Subtract the total for item 2 from the total for item 1. This is the minimum amount your disability insurance needs

to cover per month if you could no longer earn any income: $_____

4. Possible Future Expenses

If you become disabled for an extended period of time, your expenses may change over that period. Consider the following:

Education costs. If you plan to cover the costs of your child's/children's (or another dependent's) college or private education in the future, consider those costs here, particularly if your children are within five years of attending college. Knowing how much college will cost is to some degree an uncertainty because it will depend on such factors as tuition, room and board, books, and related expenses. College costs are increasing almost twice as fast as the inflation rate. SmartMoney.com and CollegeBoard.com are two great websites to help you figure out how much you should plan to save for education.

Multiply the average cost you researched, as well as any current or future costs for private education, by the

number of children. $_____

Now multiply that amount by the appropriate years before college age: 5 years: × 0.82; 10 years: × 0.68; 15 years: × 0.56; 20 years: × 0.46. The factors account for a decreasing need as you age. For example, if you planned on sending two children, one age 8 and the other age 13, to public college, you'd multiply $60,852 (the average cost at the time of writing) by 0.82 and $60,852 by 0.68, and then add the results: $49,899 + $41,379 = $91,278.

$_____

Total Potential Future Expenses: $_____

5. Assets

If you became disabled, you could turn to the assets you own to support you and your family's needs or to cover large additional expenses (such as college), primarily by selling them or liquidating them. Keep in mind that the value of your current assets may be considerably different from their value at the time you become disabled. And the values of such assets as real estate, a family business, or other big investments may be significantly discounted due to quick, forced sale or liquidation.

Bank accounts, money market accounts, CDs: $_____

Stocks, bonds, mutual funds: $_____

Retirement savings IRAs, 401(k)s, Keoghs, pension and profit-sharing plans: $_____

Equity in real estate: $_____

Current life insurance benefits that may apply to dismemberment or some other form of disability (for instance,

the ability to file a claim prior to death in the case of severe illness): $_____

Life insurance benefits (cash value): $_____

Other assets (current market value): $_____

Total Value of Assets: $_____

Take a moment to review what you've recorded on the worksheet and write down any notes that explain how you made certain determinations, such as how certain assets were valued or how you calculated certain streams of passive income. Also, if completing this worksheet helped you realize that you have few assets or savings to fall back on in case of an emergency, take some time now to begin developing a plan for building up an emergency fund of three to six months of your salary.

Notes

_____

_____

_____

_____

_____

_____

_____

_____

_____

_____

_____

_____

2 UNDERSTANDING THE TYPES OF INCOME PROTECTION THAT MAY COVER YOU

If you are like some people, you may look at the gap between your monthly expenses and income you could rely on in the event of total disability and not be too concerned. You might believe that if you did become disabled, resources such as Social Security, worker's compensation, or group benefits through your job would provide enough protection. Before jumping to that conclusion, however, you should understand the realities of the resources that may—or may not—be available to you.

Social Security Disability Insurance and Other Federal Programs

Most U.S. citizens have Social Security Disability Insurance (SSDI). The question is, will it help you?

The Social Security Administration (SSA) provides long-term disability benefits based on your salary and the number of years you have worked and contributed to the Social Security system. The SSA administers two programs that pay disability benefits: The SSDI program pays benefits to qualified individuals who are under age 65, regardless of their income when they become disabled. The Supplemental Security Income (SSI) program pays benefits only to qualified individuals with limited or no income. Only the SSDI program is discussed here. For more information on the SSI program, please go to www. socialsecurity.gov/ssi.

To qualify for SSDI, you'll need sufficient work credits earned by working and paying Social Security taxes. You can earn up to 4 credits per year, depending on the amount of your income in a year. The number of credits you need to qualify for SSDI depends on how old you are when you become disabled. For instance, if you are between the ages of 31 and 42, you'll need to have earned 20 credits within the last 10 years, ending with the year in which you become disabled. If you're younger than 31, you'll need fewer credits; if you're older than 42, you'll need more.

Social Security replaces only a limited portion of your salary, and the qualifications to receive benefits are very strict. In addition to earning enough credits, you'll need to meet all of the conditions listed below to be eligible for Social Security disability benefits:

- You must have been disabled for 5 full calendar months.

- Your disability must be expected to last at least 12 months or end in death.

- You must be unable to be gainfully employed at *any* occupation or "any substantial gainful activity," not just your occupation at the time your disability began. Generally, this means that if you are working, you cannot be earning more than $980 per month (in 2009) on average. Special rules and income limits apply if you're blind. And you must be able to prove that you cannot do the work you did before or adjust to other work because of your medical condition.

Consequently, it's fairly difficult to qualify for Social Security disability benefits. In fact, according to the 2010 edition of the Annual Statistical Report on the Social Security Disability Insurance Program, in 2009, only 34.5 percent of applications were approved (down from 56 percent in 1999). Some additional applications were approved on appeal, so the final percentage may vary from this number. Yet the sheer number of people approved every year is increasing because more and more people apply every year. Considering the current financial state of the Social Security system and future funding concerns, there may likely be fewer dollars to be distributed in coming years. In 2009, $110 billion was paid by SSDI to all disabled workers; this is more than twice the $46 billion paid in disability payments in 1999.

The SSA has a list of impairments that are considered to be so severe as to automatically designate you as disabled. If your condition is not on the list, the SSA must decide whether it's severe enough to entitle you to benefits. When determining your ability to work, the SSA will consider your medical condition, age, education, past work experience, and transferable skills. Because all of these factors must be taken into consideration, it can take more than a year for an application to be processed, and you might need legal assistance along the way, which can be costly.

If you qualify for disability benefits, certain family members can also collect monthly disability benefits based on your work record. Eligible family members may include:

- Your spouse age 62 or older, if married at least one year

- Your former spouse age 62 or older (if you were married at least 10 years)

- Your spouse or former spouse of any age, if caring for your child who is under age 16 or disabled

- Your children under age 18, if unmarried

- Your children under age 19, if full-time students (through grade 12) or disabled

- Your children older than 18, if severely disabled

Each eligible family member may receive a monthly check equal to as much as 50 percent of your basic benefit. This is in addition to your benefit—your check does not get reduced.

In addition, special disability programs are available for people with certain backgrounds or in certain industries. For instance, there are special disability programs for veterans injured in war, for railroad workers, and for miners who develop black lung disease.

All of that said, according to the 2007 Annual Statistical Report on the Social Security Disability Insurance Program (Table 43), the average monthly benefit awarded in 2007 to disabled workers was $1,054.70. That isn't much to live on. Would it cover your current monthly expenses? And could you afford to go as long as 18 months without any income or benefits while you wait to see if your application is approved? Particularly when, in the end, there is a strong chance that it won't be?

To learn more about SSDI and to read Social Security's fact sheets and actuarial publications, go to www.ssa.gov/disability.

Do you think you may qualify for any special disability programs through the federal government? If so, which one(s)?

_____

_____

What specific types of disabilities do these programs cover?

_____

_____

_____

Workers' Compensation Insurance

Workers' compensation is state-mandated indemnity insurance held by employers that covers employees for lost income and medical expenses when injuries or illnesses are work related. Workers' compensation is provided through private insurers. After a short waiting period, it may pay for your medical expenses and a portion of your lost wages. Benefits vary significantly by state and are subject to different maximum and minimum amounts. Typically, these benefits are equal to two-thirds of your pre-disability income. But because most disabilities are not work related, workers' compensation programs do not cover them. According to a July 2009 research study sponsored by the Society of Actuaries (Group Long-Term Disability Benefit Offset Study, conducted by Milliman, Inc.), only about 4 percent of long-term disability insurance claimants also receive workers' compensation benefits. While workers' compensation programs provide very important coverage to those who become sick or injured while performing the duties of their job, it does not apply in most cases of disability.

Only 10 percent of disabilities are a result of work-related injuries.

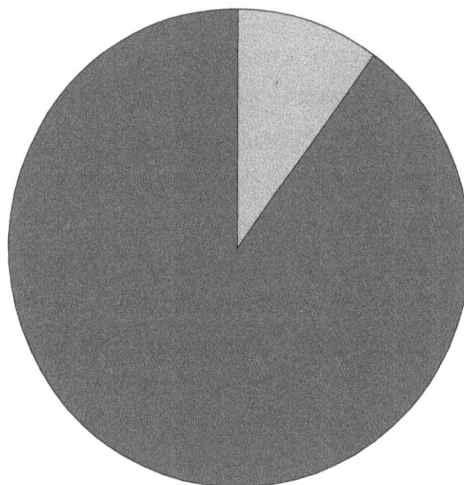

■ Not at work

■ At work

Source: National Safety Council, Injury Facts, 2004.

Based on the questions in the PDQ you filled out in step 1, do you think you have a higher than average or lower than average chance of being injured on the job? Consider the type of work you do every day and the level of risk it involves.

_____

_____

_____

State Disability Programs

Some states offer temporary disability insurance programs that can help you if you became disabled. Not every state does, however, and sometimes they apply only to certain types of workers. Likewise, most of the states that do offer some type of statutory disability insurance offer only temporary or short-term coverage, that is, less than one year. Yet if you have a disability that lasts longer than three months, there's at least a 30 percent probability that it will last five years. What will you do for the remaining four years? For a state-by-state resource guide, go to www.disability.gov/state/index?state=.

For now, let's use California as an example: California's SDI pays a weekly benefit following a 7-day waiting period. It pays for as long as 52 weeks in amounts ranging from $50 to $490, depending on the income level of the employee. The amount of the weekly benefit is calculated on a base period of earnings over a 12-month period and usually is 55 to 60 percent of earnings in the highest quarter of one's base period. The goal of the plan is to provide benefits in the event of sickness or injuries sustained off the job, when workers' compensation doesn't apply. The plan is funded by mandatory employee payroll deductions.

Your state may also offer vocational rehabilitation programs for people who become disabled, which could help you develop new skills to earn income. However, that could take some time, and you might have to recover at least partially from a disability before being ready to enter this type of program.

State government benefits can also change depending on budgetary pressures, new regulations, and so on. It may not be wise to count on your state government for coverage. For the most up-to-date information about disability insurance programs in your state, go online and search for "[name of state] disability program." For instance, for complete information on California's disability insurance program, you can go to www.edd.ca.gov/diind.htm.

Does your state have a disability program?

_____

_____

_____

How long do the benefits last?

_____

Are you covered by any special disability programs offered by your state because of your background or occupation?

_____

_____

_____

What specific disabilities are covered?

_____

_____

_____

Group Disability Insurance from Employers or Associations

If you are currently employed by a company and are eligible to receive benefits, you may have some form of disability insurance through your employer. You may also have chosen to enroll in a disability insurance program through a professional trade association or some other organization of which you are a member. Group disability insurance can be an affordable way to get income protection *and* to get different types of protection.

Your employer might provide short-term disability benefits in the form of paid sick leave, short-term disability insurance, or both. Coverage from these benefits can range from a few days to as long as a year, depending on your company's benefits and your length of employment. Short-term disability insurance benefits are typically paid when the insured is unable to perform the duties of his or her occupation (a more liberal definition of disability than for the Social Security program). Short-term disability insurance benefits are taxable (for the employee) when the employer pays the premium, which is generally the case. Some employers offer voluntary short-term disability insurance; employees may choose to participate and pay their own premiums through payroll deduction.

California, Hawaii, New Jersey, New York, and Rhode Island require employers to provide short-term disability insurance coverage with waiting periods of 7 days and a maximum benefit duration of 26 to 52 weeks, depending on the state. The maximum disability benefit amounts under these programs are typically low. The percentage of earned income covered and the maximum benefit also vary by state. Employers in these states can opt out of the state plan, obtain coverage through private insurers, or self-insure. (Basically, self-insure means that you do not purchase or obtain insurance; in other words, you retain the risk yourself.) When employers opt out, the short-term disability insurance coverage that they provide typically exceeds the statutory required minimum benefits.

Your employer may also provide group long-term disability insurance that covers you in the event of a disability (injury or illness) that lasts 3 to 6 months or longer. Oftentimes, professional trade associations will offer group long-term disability insurance programs. Long-term disability insurance usually picks up where short-term disability insurance ends.

Group long-term disability coverage replaces part of your salary if you are disabled and unable to work. (Employers may offer individual coverage also, and that almost always includes underwriting. Group long-term disability insurance is its own category.) Typically, a group long-term disability plan policy offered by your employer will guarantee that you have coverage, which means no underwriting application process is involved. A policy offered by an association or other organization will likely require an application and an underwriting process, although coverage for members of the group is sometimes guaranteed.

A typical policy through your employer replaces at least half of your salary up to a specific maximum benefit, such as $5,000 or $10,000 per month—whatever your employer decides at the time it accepts the group long-term disability insurance policy. The amount of coverage through other types of group policies can be limited and the premiums can be higher than what is available through the individual marketplace.

Benefits from group long-term disability policies generally continue until either age 65 or your retirement age under Social Security, or until you are able to return to work. In some policies, benefits may also be available for a period of time after you return to work. Most often, benefits are paid when the insured is unable to perform the duties of his or her occupation during the first two years of disability. After two years of disability, however, most plans continue to pay benefits only if the insured is unable to perform the duties of any occupation for which the employee is suited by training, education, and experience, a definition more closely resembling that in the Social Security program. Long-term disability insurance benefits are taxable to the employee when the employer pays the premium, which is generally the case, and the amount of the benefit is offset (i.e., reduced) by the amount of benefits that the insured receives from Social Security or workers' compensation. Some employers offer voluntary long-term disability insurance, where employees may choose to participate and pay their own premiums through payroll deduction. In some cases, the voluntary long-term disability insurance coverage is in lieu of coverage purchased by the employer. More frequently, voluntary long-term disability insurance coverage allows the employee to supplement the long-term disability insurance coverage provided by the employer.

Employer-paid coverage is usually not portable. In other words, if you leave the employer or the association or organization, your coverage is discontinued. If you are in good health, purchasing additional disability insurance coverage through your employer (beyond what your employer may offer and pay for) may be more expensive over any long period than purchasing an individual policy on your own because of the premiums increasing and simplified underwriting. Why? Because the underwriting—the process of determining the rate you pay based on the level of risk you pose—is not selective with group-based policies; the group policy has to cover all employees to a certain extent. But individualized underwriting is generally required if you decide to purchase more than a basic amount of coverage through the group plan. Yet the rates you pay still have to account for the generalized risk the insurance company is taking on by covering the group.

		ONLY 1 IN 3 U.S. WORKERS IN PRIVATE INDUSTRY HAS LONG-TERM DISABILITY COVERAGE THROUGH WORK		
Type of Program	All Employees	White Collar: Professional, Technical & Related Employees	Blue Collar: Clerical & Sales Employees	Service Employees
Short-Term Disability Coverage	37%	41%	42%	21%
Long-Term Disability Coverage	29%	40%	22%	11%

Source: U.S. Department of Labor, Bureau of Labor Statistics, Employee Benefits.

Finally, the Employee Retirement Income Security Act of 1974 (ERISA) governs most group disability insurance policies. This federal law offers substantially less protection to the consumer if there is a need to sue a given insurance carrier because a federal court instead of a grand jury would administer such a case. ERISA limits punitive damages in cases that are decided in the courts and allows judges the discretion to award attorney's fees. We'll discuss how this impacts the decision to get individual disability coverage in a moment (within point 3 below). For now, take a minute to fill out the questions that follow.

Do you currently have income protection—either short-term or long-term disability insurance—through your employer or a group program?

_____

_____

What are the benefits of those policies?

_____

_____

_____

_____

What are the conditions or limitations of those policies?

_____

_____

_____

_____

_____

_____

_____

3 DETERMINING WHETHER YOU NEED INDIVIDUAL DISABILITY INSURANCE AND HOW MUCH YOU MAY NEED

Now that you understand what other types of income protection may cover you in the event of a disability, you can assess your need for an individual disability insurance policy that you purchase on your own. If you are like most people, you view your chances of becoming disabled as slim. You may not receive Social Security benefits because they are difficult to qualify for and are limited. You may not qualify for the programs offered in your state. You may not have protection through your employer or another organization.

In fact, if you are like most people, when you combine your assessments in step 1 with an evaluation of possible coverage in this step, you may come to the conclusion that having your own income protection in place may be a necessity.

Individual disability insurance policies can also be used to supplement group long-term disability coverage. Why? Because individual disability insurance policy benefits are typically not subject to income tax, as the premiums are paid with after-tax dollars. Group long-term disability insurance benefits are typically taxable because the employer often pays the premiums. A few employers do offer the option to have premiums paid on an after-tax basis, in which case the benefits received are not subject to income tax.

In addition, individual disability policies typically offer more coverage because they will insure all earned income (including commissions and bonuses), whereas group long-term disability insurance plans do not usually cover commissions and bonuses and can have a maximum benefit. Individual policies also offer greater flexibility in terms of elimination period, benefit period, and optional riders in the design of the policy. And as mentioned in the previous section, even if you have the option to purchase disability coverage through your employer (where you pay the premiums), an individual policy will generally be less expensive over the long term than a group policy if you are in good health.

Recall from the discussion in point 2 that ERISA affects your ability to sue a group long-term disability insurance company. But if an individual disability insurer wrongfully denies or delays benefits, in some states you can sue for damages and emotional distress. That's important because, in many cases, if your benefits are delayed you may not be able to pay monthly bills. This can have long-term ramifications ranging from a tarnished credit report to foreclosure. The best way to maximize your benefits while avoiding ERISA regulation is by supplementing your group long-term disability insurance plan with an individual policy.

Pre-Disability Income vs. Group and Individual Policy Benefits During Disability

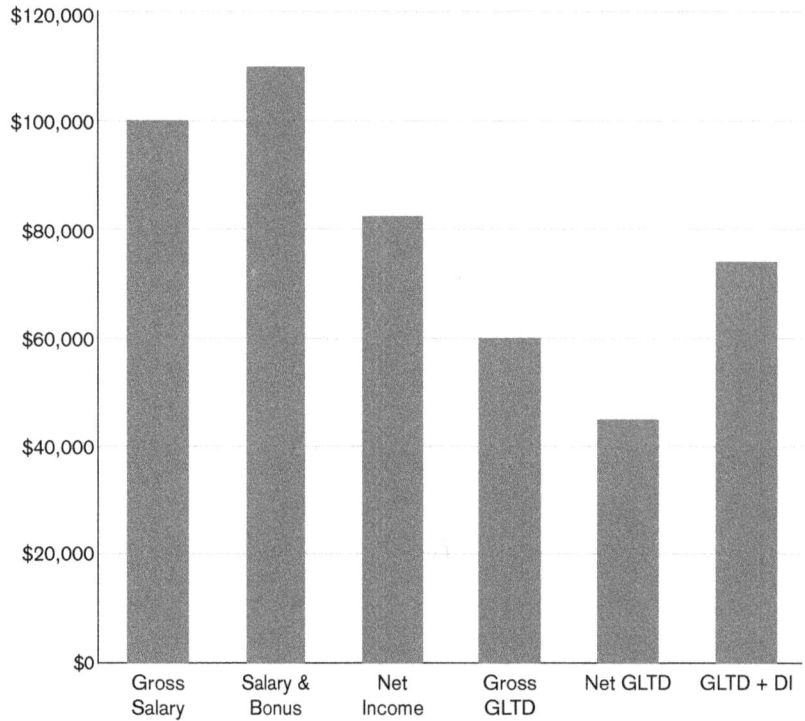

Group vs. Individual Policy Benefit Income

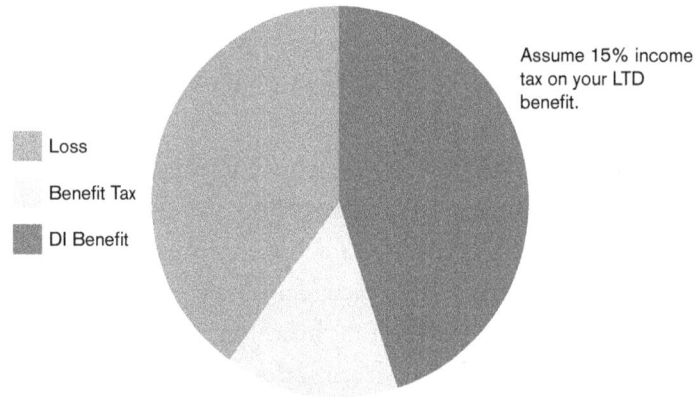

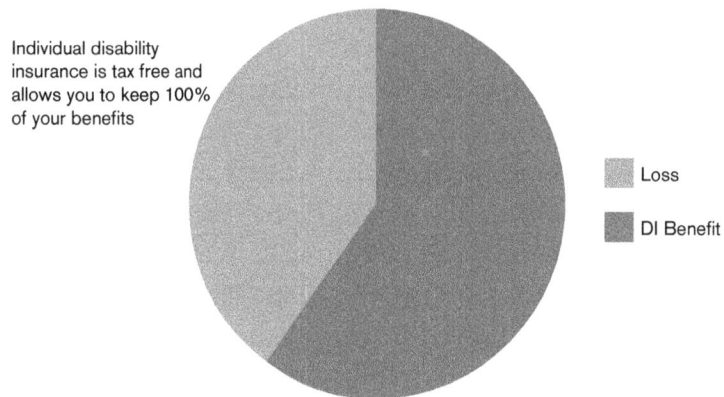

Assume 15% income tax on your LTD benefit.

Loss
Benefit Tax
DI Benefit

Individual disability insurance is tax free and allows you to keep 100% of your benefits

Loss
DI Benefit

INDIVIDUAL/GROUP DISABILITY POLICY COMPARISON		
	POLICY TYPE		
	Individual Policy	Group Policy Through an Employer	Group Policy Through an Association or Organization
Description	A policy you buy through your own insurance agent	A disability benefit you receive through your employer; your employer may pay part or all of the premiums	A disability policy purchased through an association or organization of which you are a member
Conditions	You must meet the underwriting criteria set by the insurance company for occupation, health, habits, avocations, etc.	You must be an employee of the company that sponsors the insurance	You must be a member of the association or organization (e.g., trade group) that sponsors the insurance
Advantages	Benefits are tax free if premiums are paid with after-tax dollars; you select flexible policy benefits & features, such as lifetime benefits, cost-of-living increases, etc.; provides the most comprehensive coverage; premiums generally can't increase & you generally can't lose coverage if you pay the premiums	Lower premium; both short- & long-term coverage are often available; usually you don't have to prove insurability	Lower premium; may have more liberal underwriting requirements, although coverage is not guaranteed as with employer groups
Disadvantages	Most expensive in terms of premiums	Less flexible benefit design than individual disability policies; will terminate when employment ends (non-portable); premium will often increase as you get older; definition of disability may be less liberal than with individual coverage; benefits will be offset by Social Security, workers' compensation & some other types of disability insurance	Less flexible benefit design than individual disability policies; definition of disability may be less liberal than individual coverage; contracts may be cancelable by insurance company or association; premium will increase as you get older

To fully understand your need for an individual disability insurance policy, use the following worksheet to estimate your current protection. Note that I've filled in a "sample calculation" column to help you understand the process.

	Sample Calculation	Your calculation
1. What is your annual gross income (excluding bonuses and commissions)?	$70,000	$_____
2. Do you have group long-term disability coverage? (If no, skip to item 8.)	☒ Yes ☐ No	☐ Yes ☐ No
3. What is the payout of the policy in terms of a percentage of your salary?	55%	_____%
4. Multiply the payout percentage (3) by your annual gross income (1) to determine your annual pretax benefit amount.	$38,500	$_____
5. Who pays the premiums for your group policy, you or your employer? If you pay the premiums, skip to item 8.	☐ Me ☒ Employer	☐ Me ☐ Employer
6. What is your tax bracket? (You can use 25% as a good approximation.)	25%	_____%
7. Multiply your taxable benefit amount (4) by your tax bracket percentage (6) and subtract that from the whole (4) to determine your after-tax benefit amount.	$28,875	$_____
8. What is your annual gross income, including bonuses, commissions, or other earnings not covered by your group plan?	$90,000	$_____
9. Multiply your total annual gross income (8) by 66 percent, which is a good approximation of the total individual coverage that is typically available. (Percentages will vary by policy.) If you do not have group coverage, this is an estimate of your annual individual benefit amount, which is tax free.	$59,400	$_____
10. If you have group coverage, subtract your group benefit (4 if you pay the premiums, 7 if your employer pays the premiums) from your estimated individual coverage. This would be an approximation of your individual coverage.	$27,900	$_____

Note: You may have more benefits available to you based upon your coverage, your occupation, or other types of benefits you have, but most other forms of coverage will be fairly minimal and may only apply to disabilities caused by specific events.

You now have a full understanding of the amount of the income protection you may need, the various benefits that may or may not be available to you, and how much of an individual policy benefit you might qualify for. You are now ready to dig into some of the nuances of long-term disability insurance policies to get a handle on the type of policy and the policy options that will meet your needs.

STEP 3

DISCOVER THE DISABILITY INSURANCE POLICY COMPONENTS THAT ARE BEST FOR YOU

Take a breath. Thinking about disability is serious, exhausting business. And subjecting your financial situation to an X-ray isn't always fun. But you did it—and for good measure. When it comes to disability insurance, it's important to understand your needs and what coverage you may already have if you want to get both the right coverage for you as well as the most affordable.

Now for the bad news: Many insurance companies are active in the business, and each usually offers different types of insurance products and multiple configurations. That means there's a bewildering array of options at your fingertips. It can be overwhelming, but the variability also means there is an opportunity for you to purchase the best kind of coverage for your particular circumstances. So, with disability insurance, it's critical to review the details and not make assumptions. There are thirty-plus elements in a contract, all of which can be written differently. This leads to an infinite number of possible contract variations, and each variation affects policy benefits—how much, how long, and under what terms, conditions, and circumstances a claim will be paid. However, most companies' offerings are fairly similar in the way most of the components are worded.

Now for the good news: Despite the seeming complexity, there are major similarities between all disability insurance contracts: overall, disability insurance typically works the same from company to company in that it replaces income. Buyer beware, however: the devil is in the fine print/details as to how and when the companies pay benefits.

Customizing the parameters on your policy will make a difference in the premiums (and benefits). There is no sense in being insurance rich and cash poor. Two factors are especially important here: first, to determine what you most want in a policy and the premium that you can afford and will want to continue to pay each year, and second, to use those parameters to guide your decisions.

In this step, we'll help you understand your needs and preferences in terms of the options available. That way, you are prepared, educated, and able to assess agents, insurance companies, and policies to make the best decision for you.

1 UNDERSTANDING DIFFERENCES IN CORE COMPONENTS OF THE POLICY

Every disability insurance policy has certain core definitions and parameters that can differ from company to company. These include the amount of the benefit, how disability is defined, how sickness is defined, the benefit period, and the elimination period. The following questions will help you understand what different core definitions mean to you and your situation.

Is your current salary your sole source of income?
◯ Yes ◯ No

If your salary is your sole source of income, it may be important to get the maximum **amount of coverage** you can afford. If you have passive income (such as from rental properties) that you could count on even if you were disabled, getting maximum coverage may be less important. Benefit amounts can vary from company to company, and the benefit can either be calculated as a percentage of your regular income (typical on a group policy) or be a flat amount (typical on an individual policy). Individual policies will often offer a benefit that equals 70 percent of after-tax earnings, but some may go as high as 75 percent. Working with an advisor who has access to multiple companies will allow you to obtain the maximum amount of coverage.

If you were unable to do your current job because of a physical disability, is there other work you are qualified to do (assuming you could do it if disabled)?
◯ Yes ◯ No

The **definition of disability** will vary from policy to policy. The disability definition is the most important part of the policy because everything else stems from it. Some policies pay benefits only if you are unable to perform the duties of any occupation for which you are reasonably qualified by training, experience, and education. A typical definition may read, "You are unable to perform with reasonable continuity the substantial and material acts necessary to perform your regular occupation in the usual and customary way." Other policies pay benefits if you are unable to perform the major duties of your own occupation. A feature called "own occupation" used to be common. However, depending on the definition in current contracts, it's not always necessary.

What follows is a list of different definitions of occupation that may exist in a policy:

- **Pure/True Own Occupation**—This definition allows you to be paid the monthly benefit amount, even if you are working elsewhere, so long as it is another occupation. Some carriers offer an own-occupation specialty definition. This definition might be necessary for you if you have a skill, such as being a surgeon, that could be transferred to another individual. Without this type of definition, you could be expected to teach or become involved in some related discipline within the medical field, and as a result, might not be considered totally disabled. Be careful if you have a dual occupation.

- **Transitional Occupation**—This particular definition of disability is not commonly offered. It works in much the same way as the "own-occupation" rider, but it offsets the benefit based on your new earnings. In other words, the carrier will continue to pay the benefit while you are working in a different occupation, but the benefit may be reduced by a proportion that is contingent upon your new earnings.

- **Modified Own Occupation, Not Working Elsewhere**—This definition allows you to be paid if you cannot do the duties of your occupation and are not gainfully employed elsewhere. Working, or not, then becomes the choice of the claimant.

- **Any Occupation, Unable to Work Elsewhere**—This definition will allow you to be paid only if you cannot do the material duties of your occupation and you are unable to work elsewhere by reason of education, training, and experience. (Some carriers even include prior economic status in the list of reasons.) This definition gives the carrier more control of the claim.

There can also be a variation of the above definitions in which one definition (usually own occupation) is used for a period of a few years and then another definition (usually any occupation) is used. This is less desirable to the insured because it's designed to protect the company from those who are able to return to work but prefer to stay on disability. If you returned to work and there was a loss of income, and you had a residual benefit option (you are paid if you are unable to earn a certain amount), you could be paid under the loss of earnings definition, which we'll describe later in the workbook.

Determining which type of benefit is best for you can be tricky. You should carefully consider the nature of your current occupation, how long you have been in your current occupation, and whether you've been trained for other types of work that may be less or more physical. You should also discuss the issue with your advisor.

A final component of the definition of disability is the concept of presumptive disability (this is how it is identified in the contract). All policies include a statement of presumptive disability—a level of disability that automatically qualifies you for full benefits for the complete benefit period. It usually involves the loss of one or more of the following: sight in both eyes (below 20/200); speech; hearing in both ears (not restorable with the use of a hearing aid); use of both hands; use of both feet; or use of one hand or one foot. If you suffer from these types of disabilities, you aren't required to prove the level of your disability. The insurance company presumes you will not recover.

Are you young and in good health?
Yes No

Another definition that you should check carefully is the **definition of "sickness."** It is better if the wording in the policy is "when it first manifests" rather than "when first contracted." The difference between the two is significant, especially, for example, if the disability is caused by cancer. Under the first definition, even if cancer existed when the policy was issued but it had not yet appeared or would not have caused a prudent person to seek medical attention, it would be covered. Under the second definition, it would not be covered if it could be proven to have existed prior to the effective date of the policy. This difference may not be as crucial if you are young and in good health. The chances of your having a serious illness at the time that you buy a policy are not as great when you are younger and/or in good health as when you are older and have some health concerns. Unfortunately, as we age, our risks for a variety of types of illnesses increase, and we may be ill without realizing it when we buy a policy.

Is maintaining the affordability of a policy more important to you than getting the maximum coverage possible?
◯ Yes ◯ No

When choosing your policy, you can decide what **benefit period** you want. Typically it's 2 years, 5 years, or until age 65, 67, or 70. This means that if you became disabled, you would receive benefits for 2 years, 5 years, or until you reached the specified age. Some policies even allow you to renew the policy after the stated age for 1- or 2-year periods, but you have to reapply. Obviously, the more comprehensive the coverage, the less risk you will incur. But it also comes with a higher price tag. A policy with a 2-year benefit period, for example, might cost only 15 percent of a policy that offers benefits to age 65. Working with an advisor can help you get the maximum amount of coverage at affordable rates. Still, you'll need to balance your coverage needs with your budget. It's also important to note that with group insurance policies, you cannot dictate the benefit period.

Do you have income protection for at least 6 months, either through short-term disability insurance or through money saved in liquid assets?
◯ Yes ◯ No

After a qualifying disability occurs, there is a **waiting period** before you can begin receiving benefits. This is usually referred to as an **elimination period**. The shorter the elimination period, the more costly the policy. On a group policy offered by an employer, the elimination period will usually dovetail with the benefit period for the employer's short-term disability program (to eliminate any gap in coverage, though benefit amounts may differ slightly). Elimination periods can vary from 1 month to 1 year, although 90 days is the norm. If you have short-term disability insurance or a strong emergency fund, you may want to choose a longer elimination period in order to pay lower premiums.

Is maintaining the affordability of a policy now more important to you than maintaining consistent premiums in the long run?
◯ Yes ◯ No

Today, most policies are either **guaranteed renewable** or **noncancelable.** Most policies are noncancelable in the base contract, but some insurers offer the option to make them guaranteed renewable. But what does either condition mean?

A **guaranteed renewable policy** guarantees that the insurer cannot terminate the policy as long as the premiums are paid, and the insured doesn't have to reapply at any point to continue coverage. With a guaranteed renewable policy, premiums cannot be raised based on an individual's circumstances, but they can be increased for an entire class of policyholders. No other aspect of the policy can be changed for the life of the policy, which is usually to age 65.

A **noncancelable policy** takes guaranteed renewable a step further. It offers the same parameters or protections that guaranteed renewable offers but also specifies that premiums can never be increased. Most policies today automatically include this parameter.

Nevertheless, some long-term disability policies are valid for just a certain term—usually anywhere from 1 to 5 years. After that time, they need to be renewed by the insured, which means you would have to reapply for the coverage, go through the underwriting process again, and likely pay a higher premium based upon your age. Few insurers offer it, however. It is only with special risk carriers, and that means the premiums are going to be more expensive since it is a "special risk." Policy terms leave you open to a cancellation of coverage because you have to re-qualify with medical underwriting after the expiration of each policy term. If you are found ineligible, then you will have NO coverage. It is very much in the best interest of the client primarily for that reason, secondarily for premium stability.

But here's the problem. A noncancelable policy can be substantially more expensive than a guaranteed renewable policy, as you would imagine. And when a company does offer the option to make a policy noncancelable rather than simply guaranteed renewable, the premium could be 50 percent greater. You're paying that additional cost to protect yourself against a potential, unknown, and uncertain premium increase. Yet the company may not ever increase the premium. So you need to weigh that protection against the substantial cost increase. If you have a limited budget for disability insurance, you may want to seek out an insurer that allows you to downgrade to guaranteed renewable.

2 IDENTIFYING THE ADDITIONAL POLICY COMPONENTS THAT ARE RIGHT FOR YOU

A disability policy allows plenty of options for customizing your coverage to best fit your needs. Individual policies allow you to pick and choose policy features (remember from the introduction, these are known as riders) that impact coverage and premiums. With disability insurance policies, however, there can be big differences from company to company and policy to policy in terms of which policy components are automatically woven into the policy, which are offered as optional riders, and which are not offered at all. The following questions will help you determine which configuration and policy riders would be most appropriate for you to consider.

If you could only work part-time, would you earn enough income to maintain your lifestyle?
◯ Yes ◯ No

A partial disability is one that keeps you from doing part of your job or from working full-time. A **residual or partial disability rider** covers you if you go from being totally disabled to being able to return to work part-time. With this rider, you would collect a percentage of the total benefit based on your loss of earnings. Some policies require you to be totally disabled for a period of time before the insurance company will pay a residual or partial disability claim. This is an important point to clarify. If you could not survive on part-time income, you may want to consider this rider, which may also include a recovery benefit (see below for an explanation).

Are you concerned about your ability to do other types of work if you weren't able to fulfill the duties of your current job? Or are you worried about the health of your business if you are a business owner?
◯ Yes ◯ No

The **extended/transition benefit** allows a person who is no longer under the doctor's care to be paid as if he or she was still disabled (even though he or she has returned to work full-time) as long as there is more than a 20 percent loss of income. This allows a doctor, a CPA, or a small business owner whose income or practice diminishes while that professional is disabled to return to work and still be paid while the business is being rebuilt. Benefits under this provision would continue to be paid until income reaches 80 percent of pre-disability earnings. Some companies offer this benefit for different periods of time (e.g., 12 or 24 months), while others offer it for the full benefit period (age 65). If you are the sole proprietor of or run a small business that depends on you, this may be an important benefit to consider in your policy.

Another form of an extended benefit is a **recovery benefit**. This is a lump sum paid to the claimant immediately following recovery from a partial disability. This is an extra incentive to go back to work. This lump-sum amount varies by carrier, but usually it is in the range of 3 to 6 times the monthly benefit amount; it can be less, though, depending upon how long the claimant was receiving a benefit.

Some policies have **return-to-work or rehabilitation provisions** that enable the insurer to pay for training, modifications to your work environment, or other services that assist you in returning to work. If a return-to-work policy provision is not listed, ask for the insurer's practice in this area.

Could you survive on less income than you currently earn?
Yes   No

Certain policies provide a benefit called a **lost income provision** to make up for your loss in income if you must take a lower-paying job because of your disability. If it would be extremely difficult to make ends meet if you made less than you are currently making, this provision may be important to you. (This is the duty of the partial/residual disability rider.)

Do you have savings or passive income that could cover your income needs if you had an additional waiting period in the case of a disability relapse?
Yes   No

Some policies require a new waiting period before you could begin to receive benefits in the case of a **recurrent disability**. But most policies don't require you to wait before receiving benefits if you go back to work after recovering from a disability and have a relapse within a specified period, such as 6 months.

Are you concerned about inflation?
Yes   No

A **cost-of-living adjustment or inflation benefit** provides for periodic increases in the amount paid to the insured. These usually correspond to increases in the cost of living, and they can be based upon the consumer price index (CPI) or a fixed percentage increase (e.g., 4 percent). Most carriers prefer to use the CPI. Typically this benefit commences 1 year after a claim starts to pay, but it would actually be a longer period from the point of disability when you add in the elimination period. For example, a policy with a 90-day elimination period would have a cost-of-living adjustment at 15 months.

Do you expect your income to continue to increase over time, and would you like to increase your benefit amount as your income increases?
Yes   No

A **future increase option** allows someone who is underinsured to apply for additional coverage based solely on financial underwriting, without any medical underwriting. This is especially beneficial if you were to develop health issues. This option is usually offered at certain intervals until a specific cut-off age, but keep these three different variations of a future increase in mind:

- **Optional Increase**: You may apply once per year for a coverage increase when you experience an increase in earnings.

- **Benefit Update**: This version provides an opportunity to increase coverage at predetermined intervals of time.

- **Future Purchase Option**: If you purchase an increased amount of coverage, it will come from a pool you've previously purchased.

Premiums for coverage obtained through this type of option will be based on the company's current premium schedule, the type of policy offered at that time, and your age at the time you apply for the increase. Future increase premiums are *not* based on the premiums of the original policy. This option is very important because your health is never guaranteed. No medical underwriting ensures that you will be eligible for coverage as long as you qualify financially. It may be especially important for small business owners who are still in the start-up phase and don't have a history of income in the business to prove insurability.

Do you have a family history of mental health issues or substance abuse issues or some other circumstances that increase your risk of developing these types of conditions?
Yes No

Policies usually pay benefits for a maximum of 2 years in the case of **disabilities resulting from mental health problems or substance abuse**. However, these limits usually don't apply when mental health problems or substance abuse require institutionalization. A few companies have dropped this limitation. If you are concerned about these issues, you may want to consider researching those companies that offer benefits for the full period.

Do you have financial resources that could cover your long-term care if you became severely disabled and were unable to care for yourself?
Yes No

A **catastrophic disability benefit rider** provides a monthly benefit in addition to your monthly disability benefit (and social insurance supplement, if on the policy) in the event that you become catastrophically disabled solely due to an injury or sickness and lose the ability to perform two or more activities of daily living without assistance, become cognitively impaired, or become presumptively disabled. If any of these things happen, the carrier will "presume" you are totally disabled for the rest of the benefit period. This benefit would obviously be important if you became disabled in a way that made it impossible for you to care for yourself. If you required special care for the rest of your life, do you or your family have the resources to pay for the additional costs of that care?

Long-term care insurance is usually a much more attractive alternative when considering the catastrophic rider. In general, this type of rider is more costly than a long-term care insurance policy. And long-term care insurance is usually easier to qualify for and lasts for your entire life, not just until age 65 or thereabouts.

Are you concerned about whether or not you can count on Social Security Disability Insurance if you were to become disabled?
◯ **Yes** ◯ **No**

The **supplemental social insurance rider** pays an extra benefit if you meet the insurance company's definition of total disability but not the criteria for Social Security Disability Insurance (SSDI). If you have passive income or other financial resources are available to you, this may not be an important consideration. But considering that more and more Social Security disability claims are being rejected, if you are concerned about meeting your financial needs without it, you might carefully consider this benefit. Most people purchase this supplement in order to decrease the cost of their premiums. Premiums are lower because the insurance company carries less of a risk if they know that Social Security might offset the benefit amount.

Use your answers throughout this step and the information provided on policy components to fill out the worksheet provided. Be sure to bring this worksheet with you to any meeting with an agent or an advisor and use it as a point of comparison when assessing any policy (note that you'll be given tools for that process in step 7).

Base benefit amount	☐ It is important to me to maximize my benefit amount, even if it means paying more in premiums.	☐ Maximizing my benefit amount is less important to me than keeping my premium low.
Disability/occupation definition	☐ I want to make sure that I am covered fully if I cannot perform the duties of my current job.	☐ I could potentially perform other jobs if I were to become disabled in some way, so complete coverage under my own occupation is less important to me.
Definition of sickness	☐ It is important to me that the policy cover any illness based on "when it first manifests."	☐ It is fine with me that the policy cover illnesses based on "when first contracted."
Benefit period	☐ It is important to me to maximize my benefit period, even if it means paying more in premiums.	☐ Maximizing my benefit period is less important to me than keeping my premium low & getting as much coverage as I can afford.
Waiting/elimination period	☐ I would prefer a shorter elimination period, even though it will mean higher premiums.	☐ I would prefer a longer elimination period with lower premiums.
Guaranteed renewable policy	☐ It is important to me not to have to reapply for a policy & possibly face higher premiums later in life.	☐ I'm concerned about the cost of disability insurance now & might consider purchasing a policy with a time limit to have lower premiums.
Noncancelable policy	☐ It is important to me to ensure that my premiums don't increase in the future, even if it means paying more now.	☐ It is important to me to keep my premium reasonable now, even if it means it might increase in the future.
Residual or partial disability benefit	☐ It is important to me to have a residual or partial disability benefit.	☐ It is not important to me to have a residual or partial disability benefit.
Extended/transition benefit	☐ It is important to me to have an extended/transition benefit.	☐ It is not important to me to have an extended/transition benefit.
Recovery benefit	☐ It is important to me to have a recovery benefit & as large a recovery benefit as possible.	☐ It is not important to me to have a recovery benefit.
Lost income provision	☐ It is important to me to have a lost income provision.	☐ It is not important to me to have a lost income provision.

Return-to-work or rehabilitation provision	☐ It is important to me to have a clear & strong provision for rehabilitation coverage.	☐ It is not important to me to have a clear & strong provision for rehabilitation coverage.
Recurrent disability waiting period	☐ It is important to me to have no waiting period for a disability that recurs in a given period of time.	☐ It doesn't matter to me if there is a waiting period for a disability that recurs.
Cost-of-living/inflation adjustment	☐ I would prefer that the policy stipulate a flat percentage adjustment.	☐ I would prefer an adjustment tied to the CPI, to follow inflation trends.
Future increase option	☐ I expect my salary to increase & want to explore various future increase options, even if it means higher premiums.	☐ If my salary increases in the future, I will apply for more coverage. For now, I want to keep my premiums affordable.
Mental health/substance abuse benefits	☐ It is important to me to have no limitations on mental health/ substance abuse disabilities if at all possible.	☐ Limitations on mental health/ substance abuse disabilities are not a concern for me.
Catastrophic disability benefit	☐ I would prefer to receive an additional benefit in the case of a catastrophic disability.	☐ I am not interested in receiving an additional benefit in the case of a catastrophic disability.
Supplemental social insurance benefit	☐ I would prefer to receive an additional benefit if I am totally disabled but don't qualify for Social Security disability benefits.	☐ I am not interested in receiving an additional benefit if I am totally disabled but don't qualify for Social Security disability benefits.

When considering different policy options, keep in mind that each carrier offers only certain riders per policy and may offer different riders than those listed here. And don't make a decision to add any rider too hastily. Many of these riders are more profitable for the insurance carrier than for you as the insured. The most important thing is to identify your key priorities and ensure that those priorities are met as well as possible, given what you are willing to spend on premiums.

Now that you better understand the nuances of disability insurance, it's time to explore the factors that could impact your eligibility or your premium rates.

STEP 4

IDENTIFY THE FACTORS THAT CAN IMPACT COVERAGE AND RATES

Whatever benefit configuration you've chosen, you need to be prepared for the fact that certain factors in your life, including your financial history, your occupation, and your health and medical history, will play a major part in determining whether you can obtain coverage and with which options. Before they issue a policy, most companies review these factors and consider any other disability coverage that person has. Based on this information, an insurer may offer limited or modified coverage.

Think of these factors like a credit rating. In finance the better your credit score, the more favorable your interest rate. The worse your credit score, the more you'll pony up. With disability insurance, good "credit scores" are known as **standard rates**. Certain occupations, along with good health, good medical history, and good physical fitness, can earn you good credit scores and thus better rates. This is what an insurance company likes to see. A lower credit score (i.e., riskier occupations and poorer health and fitness) results in a declined policy or a policy with limited benefits and/or exclusions, which factors in the higher level of risk an insurance company believes it's taking on to insure you. The adjustments can be significant if you are in a very risky occupation like construction work or if you have a major condition like cancer or heart disease; the adjustments can be relatively minor if you are a supervisor of manual laborers or if your height-to-weight ratio isn't optimal.

These rates are determined during the life insurance company's underwriting process, which, to stick with our credit-score metaphor, is like a "credit check" on your income, your occupation, and your health. Different insurance companies have different underwriting standards. Because the standards will determine the rates you pay, you'll want to be well aware of the standards used by the insurance company you're working with before you sign on the dotted line.

Even though standards can vary, industry-wide basic elements of underwriting for disability insurance apply in most situations. More details on the underwriting process are to come in part II, including a complete checklist/questionnaire to help you prepare for a meeting with an agent or advisor. For now, spend a few moments taking a good look at your financial eligibility, your occupational eligibility, and the health factors that could affect your eligibility, policy components, or rates.

Because the whole purpose of disability insurance is to replace your income in the event of a disability, your finances play a very important role when you are considering disability insurance. If you are considering large amounts of coverage or if the insurance you are requesting is tied to a business, insurance companies will likely ask you questions about your financial life. This is called financial underwriting. Your income and net worth compose a significant part of the underwriting process. Your income, as well as how that money is earned, will dictate the amount of coverage offered.

What an insurance company will be looking for is an insurable interest, meaning that a specific need or financial logic underlies the coverage. If someone who makes $45,000 a year requested an annual benefit of $100,000, the insurance company would question the insurable interest and would decline the case, as there would be a disincentive for the insured person to continue working. Also, when someone has assets greater than a certain amount—let's use $5 million—the insurance company would question why that person would need income protection at all. With $5 million, the individual could likely live off of that for some time or use it to earn passive income. Insurance companies are also looking for fraud.

You, as an individual applicant, may have to justify to the insurance company the amount of coverage applied for. Disability insurance companies are sensitive to the over-insurance problem—where someone is insured for a high percentage of earnings or a large benefit amount. When someone applies for a large amount of insurance, there has to be a reason why. Financial underwriting seeks to find out why, and to ensure that the amount of coverage can be justified. Therefore, the amount of coverage bears a definite relationship to the applicant's net worth and income. The underwriter needs to know the purpose of the coverage applied for. This helps the underwriter determine if the beneficiary's economic loss—in the event of the insured person's disability—is in line with the total amount of insurance inforce.

If you don't have an income history—either because you are young and just getting started in your career or because you've recently started a business or become self-employed—you'll have a hard time qualifying for coverage. If you have no income to replace, how can the insurance company justify selling you a policy? That said, some simple, low-benefit starter packages are available, and you might be able to get some form of a future increase option attached to it so that once you have a solid income history, you can increase your amount of coverage.

Answer the following questions to determine whether you meet the minimum standards to qualify for coverage.

Do you work full-time (30 or more hours weekly)?

  Yes   No

Do you work year-round (seasonal workers are not insurable)?

  Yes   No

Have you worked 6 months or more in your current job, or can you document prior experience in a related field or established contracts if you are self-employed or own a business?

  Yes   No

2 UNDERSTANDING HOW YOUR OCCUPATION AFFECTS YOUR ELIGIBILITY

Because different types of jobs come with different risk factors for disability, disability insurance companies look at your occupation closely. Even if you aren't injured on the job, certain occupations increase your risk for certain problems that can lead to disability. For instance, doing strenuous manual labor for most of your career can cause musculoskeletal problems that can lead to an injury either on or off the job.

The insurance industry breaks occupations into classes based on risk factors. That classification takes into account daily duties on the job. The better the risk factors for a class, the lower the premium. The occupation doesn't necessarily gauge the risk; rather, it gauges the nature of business. Not all insurers will cover those occupational classifications with the greatest risk.

In the following worksheet, put a check next to the description that best matches your occupation. These descriptions are based on fairly standard classifications in the disability insurance industry. Remember, underwriting may vary from carrier to carrier, and these are just common examples of what may be expected.

	YOUR OCCUPATION AND YOUR PREMIUMS	
◯	Occupations such as architects, CPAs, & attorneys	Lowest premiums
◯	Professionals & select white-collar occupations, such as school principals & bank officers	
◯	Professionals in technical or managerial positions with office duties only	
◯	Supervisors of those who perform manual duties or skilled & technical workers, such as court reporters & other clerical positions	
◯	Workers with manual labor duties; dance instructors & hair stylists also fall within this classification	
◯	The most hazardous occupations based on claim experience, including fork-lift operators, mechanics, & construction workers	Highest premiums, if covered
◯	Those in medical fields such as general practice, ophthalmology, or psychiatry	Medical fields are a separate classification; these fields have lower premiums because the risks are lower.
◯	Those in the medical fields such as surgery	Those with surgical duties are at a higher risk because the simple inability to perform surgery results in disability & so premiums are higher.

3 EVALUATING YOUR HEALTH ISSUES

Numerous health factors can impact your eligibility for coverage, your rates, or your options for coverage, including whether some conditions are covered or not.

To help you better understand your personal health factors, we've created a worksheet that presents a series of questions about existing conditions and describes the potential impact your answers may have in the underwriting process. The final decision by the insurance company will be based on whether the issue is current or in the past, the severity, the treatment, etc. Your answers on the worksheet won't give you any guarantee of coverage during an insurance company's underwriting process, but they will give you a general idea of what you can expect. Underwriting can vary from carrier to carrier; these are just some of the health issues you can expect an interviewer to ask you about. The ratings shown are additional premium charges, usually calculated as a percentage or multiple of the base premium. An experienced insurance advisor can help you sort through the process and get you the best offer from a suitable company.

PREEXISTING CONDITION		HOW IT COULD AFFECT YOUR COVERAGE & PREMIUMS		
		DECLINE	EXCLUSION	RATING
Do you have arthritis?	☐ Yes ☐ No	Possibly	Possibly	
Do you have asthma?	☐ Yes ☐ No		Possibly	
Do you have back problems or have you been treated for back problems?	☐ Yes ☐ No		Likely	
Have you had a cesarean section?	☐ Yes ☐ No		Likely	
Do you currently suffer from depression (and are being treated for it)?	☐ Yes ☐ No	Possible	Likely	0–100%
Have you been treated for depression in the past?	☐ Yes ☐ No		Possible	0–50%
Do you have diabetes?	☐ Yes ☐ No	Possible		50–100%
Do you use recreational drugs or have you been treated for drug addiction?	☐ Yes ☐ No	Likely		25%
Do you have fertility issues?	☐ Yes ☐ No		Likely	
Do you have gout?	☐ Yes ☐ No		Likely	0–50%

Do you have hypertension (high blood pressure) or have you been treated for it?	☐ Yes ☐ No				0–25%
Do you suffer from memory loss?	☐ Yes ☐ No	Likely			
Do you smoke or use tobacco products or have you done so in the past?	☐ Yes ☐ No				25%

In addition to various medical conditions, your physical fitness, specifically your weight, can impact your premiums.

What is your height? _____

What is your current weight? _____

Now, looking at the following table, use your height and weight information to find out whether your current weight will put you in a special rate category.

HEIGHT, WEIGHT, & RATINGS						
HEIGHT	WEIGHT RANGE FOR BASE RATE	RATINGS FOR WEIGHTS OUTSIDE OF RANGE				
		25%	50%	75%	100%	150%
5'0"	92–179	180	194	204	209	217
5'1"	94–184	185	199	209	214	223
5'2"	96–188	189	203	214	219	227
5'3"	99–193	194	208	219	225	234
5'4"	102–198	199	214	226	231	240
5'5"	104–204	205	220	232	237	247
5'6"	107–209	210	226	238	244	253
5'7"	110–215	216	233	245	251	261
5'8"	113–221	222	238	251	257	267
5'9"	116–226	227	244	257	263	274
5'10"	119–233	234	252	265	271	282
5'11"	122–238	239	257	271	278	289
6'0"	125–245	246	265	279	286	297
6'1"	128–251	252	271	285	292	303
6'2"	132–257	258	278	293	300	312
6'3"	135–264	265	285	300	308	320
6'4"	139–272	273	294	310	317	330
6'5"	143–280	281	302	318	326	339
6'6"	148–289	290	312	328	336	343

What Is the Medical Information Bureau?

If you have ever applied for life, health, or disability insurance, chances are you're in the Medical Information Bureau's (MIB's) database. MIB is a valuable asset to both the life insurance industry and the insurance-buying public because by helping to detect insurance fraud—which runs up claim costs, which in turn affect everyone who pays disability insurance premiums—it keeps premium costs lower.

MIB is an information clearinghouse that stores information about processing and underwriting cases gathered from more than 600 insurers. Member companies send an inquiry to MIB and receive a short, coded report with data on the applicant's medical history and other relevant underwriting information that helps the company assess the risk of the applicant. MIB carefully guards the privacy of the information in its database: only member companies may access it. All MIB member companies must agree to a strict set of standards for use of the data provided.

MIB is a taxpaying organization, supported by assessments from member insurance companies based on their total insurance in force and business written in the previous year. It is estimated that 90+ percent of the individual life insurance policies and 80 percent of the health and disability policies issued in the United States and Canada are subject to the MIB system. This is done through member companies and reinsurance treaties that nonmember companies have with member companies.

It's not a bad idea to get a peek at the information this bureau has on you. You can get an annual record disclosure without charge. Just call MIB's toll-free number: 866-692-6901 (866-346-3642 for hearing impaired). According to the MIB website (www.mib.com), here are a few things to keep in mind once you decide to submit a record request:

- If you have not applied for individually underwritten life, health, or disability insurance within the last 7 years, MIB will not have a record on you.

- You'll need to give personal identification information to help MIB locate your record, if one exists, and they may verify the identification information you provide with other consumer reporting agencies.

- You will be asked to certify under penalty of perjury that the information you provide about yourself to request MIB disclosure is accurate and complete and that you are the person who is requesting disclosure.

Upon receipt of your (a) request for a Record Search and Disclosure, and (b) proper identification, MIB will initiate the disclosure process and provide you with the nature and substance of information, if any, that MIB may have in its files pertaining to you; the name(s) of the MIB member companies, if any, that reported information to MIB; and the name(s) of the MIB member companies, if any, that received a copy of your MIB record during the 12-month period preceding your request for disclosure.

You have the right to correct any inaccurate or incomplete information that may be in the record.

How are you feeling at this point in evaluating your health? Encouraged? Discouraged? Use the space below to write out your biggest concerns when it comes to your health. That way you'll be better prepared once you meet with an insurance professional. (For more details, see the "Tips for Preparing for Your Underwriting Physical" checklist in step 7.) Also, think about which aspects of your health you can control and which you can't; write out, for your own sake, which healthy habits you can begin today—and which unhealthy ones you can discard.

Notes

Honesty Is the Best Policy

Before we leave the topic of your health, there's one more important thing you should know. It probably goes without saying, but when it comes to the underwriting process, honesty is the best policy. Don't fib about or omit details, even though you think you might be able to get a better rate if you do. And here's why (apart from the ethical considerations): It could really come back to bite you at the time when you need the coverage.

In some cases, when your disability insurance application is taken and you've sent in an initial premium payment, you'll receive a **conditional receipt**. A conditional receipt binds your disability insurance coverage effective on the date of your application provided that the underwriting process determines you are eligible for the coverage you applied for. This means that even if you are disabled the day after your application is submitted, you will be eligible to receive a limited benefit (not the full benefit applied for, typically). But if the reason you suddenly are disabled is in any way related to an undisclosed medical condition—known or unknown—that the insurer or its third-party investigator discovers during the underwriting process, *you will not receive any benefit*.

And most policies are issued with an **incontestability clause**, which means that unless you don't pay your premium, the insurance company cannot contest the insurance contract during your lifetime as long as the original policy is **in force**, no matter how your health may change. But there is almost always a window (usually for about 2 years) after the policy becomes **in force** during which the insurance carrier *can* contest the contract if there's any reason to do so, such as if it comes to their attention that you haven't disclosed a health condition.

Again, honesty is the best policy. Don't risk it.

Being honest with yourself about any health issues will help you to maximize your premium dollar. If you do have issues, having an advisor who represents multiple companies is important. Make sure the advisor discusses any potential areas of concern with a company's underwriter before you fill out an application or take any tests. Don't commit until you know the company will consider you.

Try not to get too discouraged if you're not in tiptop shape. Remember: Different insurance companies have different standards. Plus, I've found that in a significant percentage of the cases in which the initial offer from the insurance company isn't favorable, it's due to poor communication about your health. Maybe MIB's records aren't entirely accurate. Or maybe the medical director the insurance company employs during the underwriting process discovers something your own personal physician hasn't been forthcoming with you about. Or maybe the insurance carrier just hasn't been given the full picture. That's why it's so important to take a comprehensive, proactive approach to understanding your own health and the records about it that exist. And if the insurance company comes back with an exclusion, a modified coverage offer, or a declination, it's critical that you find out what that decision was based on, and if the decision is justified.

. . . .

You are now ready to begin evaluating companies and agents and working with them to select and purchase the policy and components that are just right for you.

PART II

EVALUATE AGENTS AND
COMPANIES AND PURCHASE A POLICY

STEP 5

CHOOSE AN AGENT OR ADVISOR

It's time to consider how to go about choosing a qualified disability insurance advisor to help you wade through the options best for you—if, that is, you decide to work with an advisor. I recommend it; otherwise, you won't get as objective an opinion as you'll need and assistance in obtaining the right policy for you. If, however, you are very comfortable with your understanding of the prior chapters, going to a website that offers disability insurance comparisons may seem like a viable alternative. However, since disability insurance is much more intricate than some other forms of insurance, this could be a costly error. Keep in mind that companies currently don't offer lower premiums depending on who or how a policy is obtained.

But it's not always as simple as it sounds when it comes to finding a qualified advisor.

The truth is, disability insurance historically has been sold and serviced by professionals dedicated primarily to life insurance products. In today's economy, however, even these professionals have become rare. Almost all insurance salespeople are now called by such titles as financial advisor, financial consultant, and financial planner. Consequently, not many advisors fully understand and acknowledge disability insurance—it is oftentimes overlooked.

The agent system has also changed. Years ago, almost all agents were what are called **captive,** which means they sold products exclusively for the company with which they were affiliated. Today the majority are brokers who represent multiple carriers. Some captive agents do sell other companies' products; others, however, still sell only their own products. This is important to find out and be aware of. The advisors you choose from should represent multiple companies. If they represent only one company, they can offer you only that company's products—not necessarily the best products in the marketplace or the best products for you. This is one more reason for you to shop around.

Also keep in mind that many fine people make their living selling insurance, but they depend on making sales. This can affect their recommendations. For example, oftentimes an inexpensive disability insurance policy with few riders will do the job effectively for the least cost. Yet even when a policy with fewer riders will suffice, more coverage is aggressively sold with expensive and unnecessary riders. Why? Simply because commissions are usually paid on riders. While that expensive purchase may be buying you the best coverage available, you may not actually need all of that protection.

With that in mind, here's how this step is going to work. It's fairly short and simple. First, I'm going to give you some advice on advisor referral services, which you can use to narrow down advisors in your area and give you some qualifications to look for. Then I'll provide you with some worksheets to use to help you further vet your prospective advisors before you meet with them; to help you fully prepare yourself to meet with any advisor; and to provide you with some insight on what to look for from an advisor during and after a meeting.

(1) FINDING AN ADVISOR

Any person who sells disability insurance *must be licensed*. As with an attorney needing to pass the bar in any state in which he or she intends to practice, life insurance salespeople are required to pass an exam administered by each state's department of insurance, as well as to enroll in continuing education seminars on a regular basis. *The representative you ultimately select must be licensed in the state where you, the insured, either work or live.* You can find a directory of these state departments of insurance at www. lifeinsurancesage.com. The resources and compliance standards within state insurance departments can sometimes be more lax in some states than in others. On most state insurance department websites, you can research whether or not an insurance representative is licensed.

But state licensing is just one criterion. The following organizations are two good places to start when you're looking for an advisor. (Note: Keep in mind that websites change, so if you can't find what you're looking for based on the website navigation I provide, just search for the organization name and you're sure to find it.)

Society of Financial Services Professionals (SFSP) | www.financialpro.org

The SFSP—an organization I'm proud to be a part of—started off as an alumni organization for Certified Life Underwriters (CLU) and Chartered Financial Consultants (ChFC). (More on what those terms mean in a moment.) It has since expanded to include many other types of financial service professionals.

To use the online referral service, go to the website and look for a link offering consumers help in finding a credentialed professional, or something similar. You can usually either use the name of an advisor to get full background information or enter your location to get a list of credentialed advisors near you. Be sure to select disability insurance when you're asked for a specialty. You'll get information on each advisor's designations, companies, years of membership with SFSP, products provided, and contact information.

The Life and Health Insurance Foundation for Education | www.lifehappens.org

The Life and Health Insurance Foundation for Education is an excellent organization that provides a wide variety of useful information. Their online referral service is funneled from the National Association of Insurance and Financial Advisors (NAIFA) database (www.naifa.org). While the standards are lower than those of the SFSP, their database is useful, nonetheless. Outstanding advisors are to be found through this site, and you can check out NAIFA's website to get a better understanding of their own standards.

Visit the website and look for a button or link for "Getting Coverage" or something similar. Then identify the agent menu or the "Agent Locator." Again, you can search by name or location. You should get a list of advisors and their contact information, but not their designations, so be sure to ask for those when you contact an advisor.

What Do All Those Professional Designations Mean?

Disability insurance agents may earn such professional designations as Chartered Life Underwriter (CLU) and Life Underwriter Training Council Fellow (LUTCF). Agents who also are financial planners may carry such credentials as Chartered Financial Consultant (ChFC), Certified Financial Planner (CFP), or Personal Financial Specialist (CPA-PF). These designations indicate that the agent has completed advanced training, passed rigorous exams, and is serious about professional development.

There is also a Disability Income Associate (DIA) designation, cosponsored by America's Health Insurance Plans (AHIP), the International Disability Insurance Society, and the National Association of Health Underwriters (NAHU). While the course one studies to receive this credential is fairly simple, it does demonstrate that the agent elected to focus on disability, which is pretty extraordinary. According to AHIP, people with this designation should have an "increased awareness of the risks and costs associated with disability." They should "fully understand employer-sponsored disability programs ranging from sick leave benefits to long-term disability income plans, including their tax consequences and tax planning considerations." And they should understand "how disability income insurance fits into retirement, estate, and long-term care planning."

Beware of rogue-designated advisors. The designations they "earn" can be acquired by taking simplified courses over the Internet or merely by attending a weekend seminar. In other words, these designations do not require any level of in-depth studying despite being close enough in name or sounding impressive enough to imply mastery of a certain subject. (For example, there is a page on the California Department of Insurance website [http://www.insurance.ca.gov/0200-industry/0050-renew-license/0300-cont-education/Senior-Designations.cfm—specifically Table B] that lists such designations.) This has become a source of concern for regulators and U.S. legislators. (Bottom line: if your insurance advisor doesn't have any of the professional designations I've listed above, meet with a different advisor.)

(2) PREPARING TO MEET WITH ADVISORS

While an initial meeting with an advisor may not be an in-depth analysis of your situation or needs (Why go through that over and over again?), it's best to be prepared for a variety of questions so that any advisor you meet with understands that you are educated on the subject and are able to make smart decisions based on your needs. You will also be able to discuss your priorities, and that will be important when selecting an advisor.

Bring this workbook with you and reference the various worksheets you've completed in part I. In addition, fill out the following worksheet. Note that these questions are also the questions any insurance company will ask you as part of the prescreening and application process.

Occupation Information

What is your occupation?_____

      What are your daily duties (office administrative, managerial, technical, etc.; do they involve physical labor or regular travel)?_____

Do you work for the private or public sector?_____

Are you self-employed? ◯ Yes ◯ No

      For how long?_____

      How many employees do you have?_____

      What is your percentage of ownership?_____

      Do you work in your home?_____

      If so, what percentage of your time is spent outside of the home conducting business?_____

If you are an independent contractor or business owner, what is your net income after business expenses?

_____

If you are a W-2 employee, what is your gross income?_____

Other Income Protection

Do you have any in-force coverage, through either a group or an individual plan? ◯ Yes ◯ No

If you are covered under a group plan:

      What percentage of your income is covered?_____

      What is the monthly benefit maximum?_____

      Who pays the premium?_____

If you are covered under an individual plan, what is your total monthly benefit?_____

Health Information

What is your height and what is your weight?_____

What's your tobacco usage (cigarettes, pipe, cigars, chewing tobacco, etc.)?_____

Is there anything significant about your health history?_____

What medications do you take, and for what health conditions?_____

Have you ever received counseling? ◯ Yes ◯ No

Have you ever taken antidepressants? ◯ Yes ◯ No

Lifestyle Information

Do you do any foreign travel? ◯ Yes ◯ No

    If so, where do you travel?_____

    How long are your trips?_____

    How often do you travel?_____

Have you had any significant citations on your driving record within the past 3 years? ◯ Yes ◯ No

Do you participate in hazardous sports? ◯ Yes ◯ No

Notes

_____

_____

_____

_____

_____

_____

_____

_____

_____

_____

_____

An insurance company will also want to verify your earned income, usually for the past 2 years. Earned income is primarily proven through tax documents. Why? Because earned income is not your gross or net income, it's your income after certain types of deductions. For instance:

- If you are employed and paid monthly, weekly, or hourly, your earned income is your W-2 wages minus your pretax deductions.

- If you are paid on commission (through a W-2), your earned income is your W-2 wages after pretax deductions, minus any renewal commissions.

- If you are a business owner or professional in private practice, your earned income is the amount remaining after such expenses as rents, depreciation, utilities, transportation, inventories, etc.

The type of income verification will depend on how you receive income. While you don't necessarily need to show a potential advisor this documentation, you will need to show it to the insurance company eventually, and the advisor will want to know the information, so you might as well pull it together now. The table that follows shows the required income documentation for different types of applicants with different forms of compensation.

INCOME DOCUMENTATION REQUIRED WITH INDIVIDUAL DISABILITY POLICY APPLICATION	
Student, resident, new professional	Not required
W-2 employee	—Most current 1040, including all schedules and W-2s —If income is salary only, then year-to-date pay stub showing at least 6 months of wages —If income is reported via a 1099, then most current 1040, including all schedules
Sole proprietor	Most current 1040 and Schedule C
C-corp owner	Complete W-2s & 1120, if 50%+ owner
S-corp owner	Complete W-2s & 1040, Schedule E OR Corporate Tax Return Form 1120S & Schedule K-1
Partnership owner	Complete 1040, Partnership Form 1065, Schedule K-1
LLC or LLP owner	See corresponding type of business tax return

Note that you will also have to document any unearned income from investments, rental properties, royalties, etc., that you want the insurance company to consider in calculating your coverage.

The preceding checklists and tables should help you prepare for your meeting, but you should be prepared mentally as well.

Rules for Making Smart, Thoughtful Decisions

- Make sure that you do not feel rushed through the process; a good deal will still be there tomorrow (don't delay unnecessarily, though).

- If it looks too good to be true, then it probably is.

- Practice saying NO.

- Don't sign anything until you've had adequate time to review the material.

- Inform the advisor that you need to go over the material with someone else first. If he or she discourages you from this or tells you this is a one-time deal and you have to act now, draw the meeting to a close and make an appointment to see a different advisor.

3 COMPARING AND ANALYZING INFORMATION

Use the forms provided as you conduct your research and after you come home from an initial meeting to track information on each of the advisors you are considering. I recommend that you meet with at least three potential advisors, so I've provided columns in the advisor analysis table that follows to help you compare and contrast the qualifications of three certified professionals.

Advisor 1

Name: _____

Company (if applicable): _____

Office address: _____

Office phone number: _____

Email address: _____

What services other than disability insurance does the advisor provide? _____

_____

Advisor 2

Name: _____

Company (if applicable): _____

Office address: _____

Office phone number: _____

Email address: _____

What services other than disability insurance does the advisor provide? _____

_____

Advisor 3

Name: _____

Company (if applicable): _____

Office address: _____

Office phone number: _____

Email address: _____

What services other than disability insurance does the advisor provide? _____

_____

ADVISOR ANALYSIS: EXPERIENCE, LICENSES, PROFESSIONAL DESIGNATIONS & ASSOCIATIONS

	Advisor 1	Advisor 2	Advisor 3
Last name			
Years of experience			
Employed by life insurance company or independent/part of an advisory firm? (Employed or Independent)			
Licensed with state insurance department? (Yes or No)			
Any issues noted in state insurance department's records? (Yes or No; make notes in comments section below.)			
A Certified Life Underwriter (CLU)? (Yes or No)			
A Life Underwriter Training Council Fellow (LUTCF)? (Yes or No)			
A Chartered Financial Consultant (ChFC)? (Yes or No)			
A Certified Financial Planner (CFP)? (Yes or No)			
A Personal Financial Specialist (CPA-PF)? (Yes or No)			
Do you suspect the advisor is "rogue-designated"? (see page 56)			

Additional comments:

_____

_____

_____

_____

Use the following questions to help you reflect on your meetings with advisors. Make notes in the provided space for each advisor.

1. What's your gut feeling—positive or negative? Why?

Advisor 1: _____

_____

_____

Advisor 2: _____

_____

_____

Advisor 3: _____

_____

_____

2. What happened when you told the advisor you needed to look over the material with someone else? How did he or she respond? What does his or her reaction tell you about what kind of person he or she is?

Advisor 1: _____

_____

_____

Advisor 2: _____

_____

_____

Advisor 3: _____

3. How would you rate the advisor on a scale of 1 to 5 (1 being not attentive at all to your personal needs, 5 being very attentive)?

Advisor 1: _____

Advisor 2: _____

Advisor 3: _____

4. How would you rate the advisor on a scale of 1 to 5 in terms of his or her attentiveness to your basic personal financial information, assets, and debt with regard to how that information informed his or her recommendations to you (1 being not attentive at all, 5 being very attentive)?

Advisor 1: _____

Advisor 2: _____

Advisor 3: _____

5. Was the advisor's information-gathering process thorough? Did he or she seem to weigh in on your specific needs or simply give a cookie-cutter pitch?

Advisor 1: _____

Advisor 2: _____

Advisor 3: _____

6. How did you feel about the costs of any policies discussed? Did the potential premiums look like they'd fit your price range?

Advisor 1: _____

Advisor 2: _____

Advisor 3: _____

7. Was the advisor able to adequately and concretely demonstrate the workings of each policy and to explain what everything on any proposals or illustrations meant? Explain.

Advisor 1: _____

_____

_____

Advisor 2: _____

_____

_____

Advisor 3: _____

_____

_____

8. Did the advisor seem honest, authentic, transparent? If the attention was more on you and your needs than selling you a policy before you walked out the door, it's a good sign. If the advisor didn't know an answer to your question, did he or she weasel out of it or admit not knowing the answer? Did he or she promise to research the issue and get back to you with an answer? Explain your general experience with the advisor in this regard.

Advisor 1: _____

_____

_____

Advisor 2: _____

_____

_____

Advisor 3: _____

_____

_____

9. Basic litmus test: If five friends asked you to recommend a disability insurance advisor, would you recommend this person?

Advisor 1: _____

Advisor 2: _____

Advisor 3: _____

Use this space to remark on the general pros and cons of the advisor or anything else you've found during your research or your initial meeting.

_____

_____

_____

_____

_____

_____

_____

_____

_____

_____

_____

_____

_____

_____

Choosing an advisor may be the most challenging decision you make. When getting recommendations, consider the source carefully. For instance, if a well-known estate planning attorney refers someone to you, that should probably carry more weight than a recommendation from someone you run into playing tennis or from a friend or relative of the person who's being recommended. Just because an agent or advisor is referred by someone you know doesn't mean he or she is qualified. If this doesn't make sense, think Bernie Madoff!

Once you select an advisor, you're ready to turn your attention to the insurance companies themselves.

STEP 6

SELECT A DISABILITY INSURANCE COMPANY

You understand your needs and you've selected an advisor. You're done, right? Well, maybe. If you've done your due diligence, your advisor should be steering you in the direction of the best policy at the best rate to meet your needs. But that doesn't mean you shouldn't continue to be an educated consumer.

So, where to begin? You could either research companies you think you might like to work with before your advisor makes recommendations, or you could wait for your advisor's recommendations and then research the companies carefully. Either path is fine. But one way or the other, you should do your own research. But how?

My rule of thumb if you are starting on your own is simply to identify the top-rated companies that offer the particular type of policy you are looking for. This is good information to have even if you are working with an advisor. If your advisor doesn't recommend one of these companies, you should find out why.

The key to breaking through the clutter of the vast array of options (insurance companies, remember, can have more than one product to offer you) is to hold each company to this set of benchmarks:

1. Does the company have one of the **top tier rating**s—1st, 2nd, 3rd, sometimes 4th highest—from one or more of the independent companies that rate life insurance providers?

2. Does the insurance company hold itself to any official ethical standards?

3. How many complaints—and of what nature—are filed against the company in question?

Here's the deal I'll make with you. In this step, I'll give you the tools and resources to research each of these benchmarks if you'll put in the legwork. Sound good? I'll start by providing the resources in the order of the benchmarks I've listed above, and then the remainder of the step will consist of a set of worksheets you can use during your research on each company. You could start by visiting these resources and determining your choices from there, or you can do some of your own online research and use these resources to effectively grade the companies you've singled out as viable options. It's up to you.

1️⃣ FAMILIARIZE YOURSELF WITH THE AGENCIES THAT RATE DISABILITY INSURANCE COMPANIES.

A **rating** is just a way for the big four rating agencies—A.M. Best, Fitch, Moody's, and Standard & Poor's—to express their independent judgments of a disability insurance company's financial soundness and creditworthiness. Each agency's rating system varies in its stringency and its methodology, but all four consider a company's financial leverage, management stability, recent performance, overall financial health, and such external factors as competition, diversification, and market presence. Each company does weigh each component differently. Don't worry too much about the details here; suffice it to say that an insurance company with a top rating from at least three of the four agencies is in great standing.

You might think that large, respected disability insurance companies are exempt from financial meltdown. But they're not. That's why it is so important to consider the financial well-being of a disability insurance company before you commit.

At the end of this step (on pages 73–74) is a detailed worksheet that you will complete with the relative ratings for the companies you are considering.

DEEPER INSIGHT

Comparing ratings from each rating agency is a reliable way to evaluate insurance providers. For the financially savvy who can tease apart complex financial reports and want to review more advanced evaluations of a provider's financial health, such as financial analysis, Insurance Regulatory Information Reports (IRIS), and Risk Based Capital (RBC) system, refer to www.lifeinsurancesage.com.

What follows is a snapshot of the nature of each rating company and a look at what their top tiers of rating categories mean. For more detailed information about how to use advanced financial information on these websites, please go to www.lifeinsurancesage.com. Websites change a lot, so keep looking—the information's there. Also note that you'll need to establish free accounts for some of these services.

A.M. Best Company | www.ambest.com | 908-439-2200

A.M. Best is the most experienced rating insurance company, having been in the business since 1906. Their Financial Strength Rating is recognized worldwide as the benchmark for assessing and comparing insurers' financial stability.

To enhance the usefulness of ratings, A.M. Best assigns each rated (A++ through D) insurance company a financial size category (FSC). The FSC is designed to provide a convenient indicator of the size of a company. All that means is that you'll have additional peace of mind that the company you're dealing with is healthy.

Following is a description of what the top ratings mean:

- **A++ and A+ (Superior)**—Assigned to companies that have, in A.M. Best's opinion, a superior ability to meet their ongoing obligations to policyholders.

- **A and A- (Excellent)**—Assigned to companies that have, in A.M. Best's opinion, an excellent ability to meet their ongoing obligations to policyholders.

- **B++ and B+ (Good)**—Assigned to companies that have, in A.M. Best's opinion, a good ability to meet their ongoing obligations to policyholders.

Fitch | www.fitchratings.com | 800-753-4824

- As with other forms of national ratings assigned by Fitch, national insurer financial strength ratings also assess the ability of an insurer to meet policyholder and related obligations relative to the "best" credit risk in the country for which the rating appears, across all industries and obligation types. On the website, you'll find a detailed business review and overall outlook for the company, if you're interested in digging deeper.

Following is a description of Fitch's top ratings:

- **AAA**—Assigned to companies that, in Fitch's opinion, have the highest rating within the national scale for a particular country. The rating is assigned to the insurance entities' obligations to their policyholders, with the lowest credit risk relative to all other obligations or issuers in the same country, across all industries and obligation types.

- **AA**—Assigned to companies that, in Fitch's opinion, have a very strong capacity to meet policyholder obligations relative to all other obligations or issuers in the same country, across all industries and obligation types. The risk of ceased or interrupted payments differs only slightly from the country's highest-rated obligations or issuers.

- **A**—Assigned to companies that, in Fitch's opinion, have a strong capacity to meet policyholder obligations relative to all other obligations or issuers in the same country, across all industries and obligation types. However, changes in circumstances or economic conditions may affect the capacity for payment of policyholder obligations to a greater degree than for financial commitments denoted by a higher-rated category.

CONFLICT OF INTEREST?

In most cases, disability insurance companies must pay a fee to be rated by one of the big four rating agencies. And sometimes these fees are pretty steep–tens of thousands of dollars even. If you're inclined to think this setup might affect the objectivity of the rating agency, don't worry: A rating agency depends upon its reputation. It wouldn't be in business without it, though after the latest financial crisis, this has been a subject of debate and there have been hints of some other type of federal rating entity.

Moody's | www.moodys.com | 212-553-0377

Moody's insurance financial strength ratings are opinions of the ability of insurance companies to punctually repay senior policyholder claims and obligations. Following are descriptions of their top ratings:

- **Aaa**—Assigned to companies that, in Moody's opinion, offer exceptional financial security. While the credit profiles of these companies are likely to change, such changes are unlikely to impair their fundamentally strong position.

- **Aa**—Assigned to companies that, in Moody's opinion, offer excellent financial security. Together with the Aaa group, they constitute what are generally known as high-grade companies. They are rated lower than Aaa companies because long-term risks appear somewhat larger.

- **A**—Assigned to companies that, in Moody's opinion, offer good financial security. However, elements may be present that suggest a susceptibility to impairment sometime in the future.

Standard & Poor's (S&P) | www.standardandpoors.com | 212-438-2400

- Standard & Poor's insurer financial strength rating is a current opinion of the financial security characteristics of an insurance organization with respect to its ability to pay its insurance policies and contracts in accordance with their terms. This rating is based on information furnished by rated organizations or obtained by the rating company from other sources it considers reliable. S&P does not perform an audit in connection with any rating and may on occasion rely on unaudited financial information. On the website, you'll find a fairly detailed report that you can review for any particular company.

Following is a description of their top ratings:

- **AAA**—Assigned to companies that have, in S&P's opinion, extremely strong financial security characteristics.

- **AA**—Assigned to companies that have, in S&P's opinion, very strong financial security characteristics, differing only slightly from those rated higher.

- **A**—Assigned to companies that have, in S&P's opinion, strong financial security characteristics but are somewhat more likely to be affected by adverse business conditions than are insurers with higher ratings.

Here's a glimpse of each agency's rating system side by side. Remember: You're looking for a company with a top rating with at least three of the four agencies.

RANK	A.M. BEST	FITCH RATINGS	MOODY'S	STANDARD & POOR'S
1	A++ (Superior)	AAA	Aaa (Exceptional)	AAA (Extremely Strong)
2	A + (Superior)	AA (Very Strong)	Aa (Excellent)	AA (Very Strong)
3	A (Excellent)	A (Strong)	A (Good)	A (Strong)
4	A- (Excellent)	BBB (Adequate)	Baa (Adequate)	BBB (Good)
5	B++ (Good)	BB (Fairly Weak)	Ba (Questionable)	BB (Marginal)
6	B (Fair)	CCC	Caa (Very Poor)	B (Weak)
7	B- (Fair)	CC	Caa (Very Poor)	CCC (Very Weak)
8	B- (Fair)	CC	Ca (Extremely Poor)	CC (Extremely Weak)
9	C++ (Marginal)	C	C	R (Under Regulatory Supervision)
10	C+ (Marginal)			
11	C (Weak)			
12	C- (Weak)			
13	D (Poor)			
14	E (Under Regulatory Supervision)			
15	F (In Liquidation)			
16	S (Rating Suspended)			

2 DETERMINE IF THE DISABILITY INSURANCE COMPANY ADHERES TO AN OFFICIAL SET OF ETHICAL STANDARDS.

Each carrier adheres both to its own ethical practices and to basic guidelines dictated by each state's respective insurance department. (You can find a directory of each state's insurance department at www. lifeinsurancesage.com.) If you can't find the insurance company listed among your state's insurance department records, run the other way.

3 CHECK TO SEE IF ANY COMPLAINTS HAVE BEEN FILED AGAINST THE DISABILITY INSURANCE COMPANY.

Every company—insurance or otherwise—has complaints against it. And the Web makes it exponentially easier for all of us to air our grievances. Because most disability insurance carriers aren't going to have spotless records, the trick is for you to see how many complaints have been logged against them and of what nature. If, for example, you find that a company has multiple, recent, frequent complaints that indicate they're uncomfortably aggressive during a policy's initial contestable period (usually the first 2 years), there may be cause for concern. The same goes for its looking like claimants have a particularly tough time receiving benefits promptly (and having claims approved).

Each state's department of insurance maintains data on the number of complaints filed against an insurance company, as well as pending class-action lawsuits. To find your state's department of insurance, visit www.lifeinsurancesage.com or go to the website of the National Association of Insurance Commissioners (NAIC) at www.naic.org. And run an online search for the name of the company to see if any complaints exist on unofficial sites.

4 COMPARE YOUR RESULTS.

Use the worksheet shown on the next page to record information as you're researching various disability insurance companies. Feel free to take the setup from these worksheets and create your own if you decide to substantively research more companies. Answer the questions in the "Ratings" category of the worksheet the best you can.

The financial strength of a disability insurance company is highly important because a disability insurance policy is a long-term investment. Disability insurance companies are evaluated by ratings agencies, which assign ratings based on a company's financial strength and ability to meet obligations to policyholders. Some insurance companies are not rated by all of the rating services. (For further information on ratings and contact information for the rating services, please visit the ratings area on my main website at www.lifeinsurancesage.com.)

Now that you have an advisor and have identified companies you want to work with, it's time to apply for and purchase a policy.

	COMPANY A:	COMPANY B:	COMPANY C:	COMPANY D:	COMPANY E:
Website/ Phone					
A.M. Best Rating					
Fitch Rating					
Moody's Rating					
Standard & Poor's Rating					
Total Admitted Assets					
Total Liabilities					
Separate Accounts					
Total Surplus & AVR					
5 Yr Investment Yields					
Total Income					
Net Premiums Written					
Net Operating Earnings					
Notes: Complaints, etc.					

STEP 7

SELECT A POLICY AND COMPLETE
THE APPLICATION PROCESS

Now that you have identified an advisor and have a much better idea of what a qualified provider looks like, you're ready to make a big step forward: evaluating and purchasing a disability insurance policy.

Even if you are working with an advisor, selecting a policy and preparing yourself for the underwriting process is ultimately up to you. But in this step, I offer tools to help you compare and select a policy and a checklist for completing the application process, including tips for preparing for your physical.

(1) COMPARE AND SELECT A POLICY

It's time to begin assessing policies. Your agent or advisor should present you with more than one policy to consider. Use the following table to evaluate your options.

COMPARE YOUR PROPOSALS WORKSHEET

Product Feature	POLICY A		POLICY B	
	Amount/ Options/ Limitations	Premium	Amount/ Options/ Limitations	Premium
What is the base benefit amount?				
What is the definition of disability (or occupation coverage), including definitions of presumptively disabled?				
What is the definition of sickness?				
How long is the benefit period?				
What is the waiting (elimination) period)?				
Is the policy noncancelable?				
Is the policy guaranteed renewable?				

	POLICY A		POLICY B	
Residual/partial disability benefits				
Extended/transition benefit				
Recovery benefit				
Lost income provision				
Return-to-work or rehabilitation provision				
Recurrent disability waiting period				
Cost-of-living adjustment				
Future increase (automatic or not) or purchase option				

	POLICY A		POLICY B	
Mental health/substance abuse benefits				
Catastrophic disability benefit				
Supplemental social insurance benefit				
Other riders offered				
Other exclusions				
Company: A.M. Best Rating				
Company: Fitch Rating				
Company: Moody's Rating				
Company: Standard & Poor's Rating				

② COMPLETE THE APPLICATION PROCESS

The most important thing to remember during the application process is to fill out your application accurately and completely. This is where being prepared and taking it step by step can be very important. Always answer questions truthfully and with as much background information as possible. It's better to err on the side of disclosure than not disclosing. If a question is not answered accurately, it may be grounds for the company to not pay benefits and to cancel coverage.

Follow this step-by-step checklist to make sure you cover all bases.

1. Compile a list of all physician and medical group names. Be sure to include contact information, dates consulted, and purpose/outcome for each. Also include a list of all prescription and nonprescription medications and their dosages, as this information may be needed for the application, exam, or personal history interview.

2. Compile all required financial documentation.

3. Complete your application and any required forms. Most companies will offer conditional or limited coverage up to a set amount of coverage before the actual policy initiation date if you've evidenced insurability.

4. Submit your application to the disability insurance company for underwriting consideration. This will typically take 4 to 6 weeks, but it can take months if you're requesting a large amount of coverage and/or if you have a complex medical history.

5. Prepare for your physical. (Review the "Tips for Preparing for Your Underwriting Physical" on the following page.) Most insurance companies require some type of paramedical exam during the application process; this usually consists of a height/weight check, blood pressure check, and blood and urine specimens. The exam is often more comprehensive at older ages and for larger amounts of coverage and can include a more thorough exam by a medical doctor. (Again, consult the checklist for tips on how to prepare for a medical exam.)

6. Order your medical records. This can take 3 to 4 weeks depending on your physician/medical group.

7. Prepare for a personal history interview. This is a phone interview done through a third party that verifies information provided on the application and paramedical exam and additional questions from the underwriter. The company is making sure that all questions are answered consistently. Make sure you've got your ducks in a row on this one.

8. Complete any additional questionnaires. These are often required for specific medical conditions and hazardous work-related activities and hobbies.

9. Brace for any modifications or ratings. Remember, there are thousands of disabling illnesses and injuries. One or two exclusions are not necessarily a reason to refuse a

policy. This may not be a big deal at the end of the day.

10. Make the final decision. After the underwriting steps are completed, either an offer of coverage will be made or coverage will be declined. If your application is modified or rejected, make sure it's crystal clear to you why you were not offered the coverage you specifically applied for. Sometimes miscommunications regarding your health (e.g., inaccurate health records), finances, or occupation could hamper your acceptance.

11. Choose the mode of premium payment. If your application is accepted, you'll need to select the premium mode, or how often you pay your premium. Almost always, you have a choice of paying premiums monthly, quarterly, semiannually, or annually. Insurance companies typically charge more when you pay other than annually. Changing how often you pay your premium could save you money (it may be a lot!).

Note that underwriters base their decisions on the information received, and sometimes they can change their decisions when additional information is provided and reviewed. And remember that different companies treat some specific conditions differently, so your rate classification can vary from company to company. If you've been denied coverage, or if you're not happy with an offer, you should consider a second opinion.

TIPS FOR PREPARING FOR YOUR UNDERWRITING PHYSICAL

I'm no physician, but here are some medical underwriting tips based on my long experience in this industry and my many discussions with underwriters. Bookmark this checklist and work through it when your examination draws near.

Relax. Insurance companies are looking for average people, not superhumans.

Watch what you eat. It's best not to eat for 8 hours prior to the examination and to avoid caffeine. Schedule a morning examination if at all possible, when you're more likely to be relaxed. Being relaxed helps produce positive readings of blood pressure and electrocardiogram (EKG) levels.

Avoid alcohol. Alcohol tends to elevate blood pressure for 12 to 24 hours. Avoid drinking alcoholic beverages for at least 24 hours prior to the examination.

Get a good night's rest before the exam.

Give a urine specimen before a blood pressure check. The elimination of fluids tends to moderately lower blood pressure.

Avoid smoking. If you are a smoker, don't smoke at all within 30 minutes of the exam. Smoking tends to elevate blood pressure by constricting the artery walls.

Avoid salt. Salt retains fluids. Avoid it or use it very lightly for 3 or 4 days prior to the examination. This can have a beneficial effect on your blood pressure.

Discuss any potential problems with your advisor prior to the examination. This can affect your advisor's recommendations, such as which company or companies to apply to and how to prepare for the underwriting process. The advisor might want to discuss your case informally with the underwriter before you apply. In some cases, this can be beneficial. Also be certain the examiner correctly lists the location of doctors and hospitals that you have seen in the past, since the insurance company will most likely request their reports.

Now you're all set. But policies by no means begin and end at the dotted line. From this point forward, we'll be looking at how to monitor in-force policies after you make your purchase (and what to consider when deciding to replace a policy or terminate it altogether), along with the very important topic of filing a claim.

PART III

UNDERSTAND, MAINTAIN, AND MONITOR
YOUR POLICY OR MAKE A CLAIM

STEP 8

ASSESS, MONITOR, AND
UPDATE YOUR POLICY

Disability insurance doesn't end when you purchase a policy. Policies are living things, and many components can affect their performance. Plus, your needs may change over time. To ensure that you have all of the income protection you need, you must learn to monitor your policy carefully. At the end of this step, we've provided a worksheet that will help you track key information related to your policy and will provide a quick reference for you to look at once a year to remind yourself of important details.

MONITORING YOUR POLICY

One important factor to be aware of is the possibility of future premium increases. A noncancelable rider guarantees stable premiums. On the majority of individual disability insurance policies, this rider is automatically included, so your premium is likely guaranteed. That can assist you in your overall budgeting. However, it may not be included. You must keep that in mind so you can budget for possible increases.

Other considerations to monitor besides the premium include the ones described in the following paragraphs.

Exclusion Reviews for Removal

Oftentimes, an individual disability insurance policy is issued with exclusions for a certain conditions, such as an exclusion for a recent wrist injury. If a condition is excluded, any disability resulting from that injury or illness would not be covered. These exclusions can sometimes be removed after a certain period. Sometimes the company will indicate that period of time when a policy is issued, and other times, it needs to be brought to the company's attention for consideration. This is why it is important to monitor your policy and be proactive. An exclusion will be removed only if there has been no recurrence of the original issue. Some exclusions cannot ever be removed.

It's important to note that it will be entirely up to you to pursue changes to your policy or to get an exclusion removed. Even if there is a timeline set for the exclusion, don't assume that your insurance company will automatically remove it. Make a note to contact them at the end of the set period to make sure that the exclusion is removed.

When you contact the company to ask that an exclusion be removed, they may ask you to provide proof that there has been no recurrence of the injury or any ongoing health issues related to the exclusion. Be prepared to provide medical information to back up your request.

Future Purchase Option

As discussed earlier in the workbook, if you have a future purchase option attached to your policy, you can purchase additional coverage without evidence of insurability (medical underwriting) at certain time intervals, if your income has increased. The premium for this new coverage is based on rates available when this option/rider is exercised. It usually works in one of the following two ways: For some policies there is a "pool," or total amount, that becomes available based on your new increased earnings. Another variation does not include a predetermined "pool"; instead, it offers the opportunity to increase coverage within 90 days of an earnings increase. The carrier will request updated income documentation and make an offer for increased coverage based on your new higher earnings. On other policies, it comes at a set amount each time (for example, $500 of monthly benefit) and is on a use it or lose it basis—in other words, it cannot be accrued.

Future Increase Option (FIO)

The future increase option rider purchases additional coverage at certain points in the contract. The policyholder reserves the right to increase the coverage by paying the extra premium or they can waive it. It is a good idea to talk to your insurance agent any time you receive an increase in annual earnings so that your agent will know whether or not it is an appropriate time to exercise the FIO.

ACTION STEP TRIGGERS FOR FIO

You may have an opportunity to increase your disability insurance coverage without any medical underwriting, regardless of health. These terms are based on the definitions of the Future Increase Option (FIO) feature of your policy and are usually reserved for policyholders under age 50. Much like your initial search for disability insurance coverage, the amount available to you is tied to your earnings. Some policies require you to notify the carrier within 90 days of an increase in earnings. Other types of policies will allow you to trigger the FIO on policy anniversary dates only. That is why it is a good idea to talk to your insurance agent anytime you receive an increase in annual earnings so that your agent will know whether or not it is an appropriate time to exercise the FIO.

If it is an appropriate time to add coverage, then your insurance carrier will send you a quote for the increased coverage after you inquire about an increase. They may ask for your current earnings in order to provide an accurate quote. The carrier will usually send an FIO application along with the quote for increased coverage. The application is usually much more simplified and contains no medical questions. It is your responsibility to complete the application and submit the requested income verification along with the application (this may include a W-2, 1040, 1099, P&L, or a just a simple year-to-date pay stub). The carrier will review the application, complete the quick financial underwriting process, and then send you a notice of approval or declination based on those two criteria.

To help you monitor the various aspects of your policy, we've provided the following worksheet. Record the details of your policy and make notes about when to follow up with the insurance company.

DISABILITY INSURANCE POLICY MONITORING WORKSHEET

	SAMPLE DETAILS	YOUR DETAILS	NOTES FOR MONITORING
Carrier	XYZ Life Insurance Company		
Policy Number	12345678		
Issue Date	6/13/2011		
Monthly Benefit	$8,280		
Premium Mode	Semi-Annual		
Modal Premium	$1,969.94		
Premium (if switched to annual)	$3,817.70		

	SAMPLE DETAILS	YOUR DETAILS	NOTES FOR MONITORING
Annualized Current Premium	$3,939.88		
Annual Savings (if switched to annual)	$122.18		
Elimination Period	90 days		
Maximum Benefit Period	60 months		
Riders	—Partial Disability —Indexed Cost of Living —Future Purchase Option— Note: contact XYZ company in June 2014		
Noncancelable or guaranteed renewable or other?	Noncancelable		
Exclusions	Broken left ankle—Note: contact XYZ company for review in June 2013		
Questions to ask regularly: Has my income increased since I purchased coverage? Have I lost any other coverage, such as group coverage?			

TERMINATING OR REPLACING A POLICY

An individual disability insurance policy can easily be terminated. Usually all it takes is a phone call to the insurance company. However, keep in mind that once a policy is terminated, it's terminated. Some companies may offer a short reinstatement period, but not all will. Also, newer coverage is most likely going to come at a much higher cost, require underwriting, and have policy definitions that may not be as liberal. If you're terminating due to a cash crunch, you may want to consider making changes to the policy rather than terminating it straight out. Modifications that can reduce your premium include removing riders, reducing coverage, increasing the elimination period, and shortening the benefit period. But keep in mind that these modifications, once made, are permanent and cannot be undone. Your policy may feature the ability to make other modifications, so read it carefully and review with your advisor and/or the company. They may have other useful suggestions.

Terminating a group disability policy may be a different story. This coverage—at least the base coverage—frequently cannot be terminated because all employees are insured. If you've purchased supplemental coverage, you may be able to modify it as described above. But you may have to wait until your open enrollment period to make any changes. This is common in group plans.

If you have opted into group coverage through an association, it may be easier to cancel it if you need to.

Replacing a policy is not usually recommended, as older policies are usually lower priced and have more liberal policy definitions. If a new policy does make sense, make sure the new policy is in place prior to terminating an existing policy. But think twice before replacing a disability insurance policy. It usually does not make sense.

. . . .

By understanding, maintaining, and monitoring your policy, you will avoid any unpleasant surprises in the future and ensure that you will have sufficient coverage when you need it.

STEP 9

FILE A CLAIM

We all buy income protection policies with the hope that we never have to use them. But many of us will have the misfortune of enduring a disabling event. If that happens, you may be left thinking, "What do I do next?" It's common to look to your insurance agent to help the process along the most efficient path. Perhaps your agent will want to guide you through the claims process, which is great. But the most effective thing you can do is to immediately get in contact with the carrier—specifically their claims department.

Your carrier's claims department will ask you a series of questions to gather enough relevant information in order to trigger the claims process. Sometimes, depending upon the carrier, you may have to provide current written notice of the claim and financial documentation such as a tax return or a pay stub in order to prove that you are actually enduring a financial burden due to disability. They may also request verification of such additional information as your occupation, daily duties, and the amount of hours you work per week.

The claims department will also request additional information after your initial conversation with them. Of course they would not begin to pay a claim without the proper notations from your doctor, so plan on alerting your doctor about your disability policy so he or she is prepared to send the required medical information to the carrier. This process verifies your claim and explains that you in fact incurred an accident or sickness, and your inability to perform your occupational duties is sufficient to meet the definition contained in the policy you chose to purchase.

After your conversation with the claims department, you will be asked to fill out a claims form. This is usually a short document provided by your disability insurance carrier. This form, along with any other income documents and medical notes, must usually be submitted to the carrier within 30 days of the point of initial contact. Your carrier's claims department will typically take a week or two to process these forms.

Claims through a group disability policy or any other policy that offsets against legislated benefits will also require you to apply for any and all social benefits for which you may be eligible. This may include, but is not limited to, Social Security DI benefits, workers' compensation, and state DI programs.

Your benefit payments will start coming to you once you've completed all the necessary steps above and satisfied your waiting period. Your first check will arrive a month after the "commencement date," which is the first day immediately following completion of the waiting period. Some carriers may require a "continuance of disability form" to be completed each month, while others simply require a renewed evaluation from your doctor every few months.

An important note to people who currently have older policies, purchased prior to 2005 or so: Until the last 5 years, insurers included in their policy contracts a stipulation that if your income was lower when you become disabled than it was when you purchased the policy, the benefit amount would be lowered. Carriers have abandoned this practice lately, but if you hold an older policy, you should check to see if this is the case.

RELATION TO EARNINGS CLAUSES

Many older policies, and some current ones, contain what is known as a "relation of earnings to insurance clause," or a "relation to earnings clause." This easy-to-miss language broadly states that the insurance company reserves the right to review your earnings at time of claim and withhold any amount that they would consider to be "over-insurance."

For instance, someone applies for disability insurance coverage while earning $100,000. This typically results in a monthly benefit amount of $5,000. This equates to $60,000, or 60 percent of the insured's pre-disability earnings. However, if the insured's income drops to $70,000 in a down year, and the insured needs to file a claim that same year, then the insurance company can reconsider the $5,000/month benefit amount and instead send a monthly check for $3,500, which is 60 percent of the insured's earnings at time of claim.

In other words, this particular insured was paying for a benefit amount of $5,000 per month, but only received $3,500 per month. If the insured had known that this would be the case, then she might have decided to change the coverage amount in order to save money on her premium.

Most "relation to earnings" contracts are off the market. Today's policies will send a benefit amount of the agreed amount (in this case that would be $5,000 per month). However, it would be wise to review the terms of a relation of earnings to insurance clause if you have an older policy.

One thing to consider when making a claim is the tax consequences of that claim. **Please note that the following is not tax advice and you should consult your tax advisor if you have questions.** The tax consequences of a claim vary from policy to policy and are usually dependent on who pays the premium, as we discussed in step 2. The general rule is that, on an individual disability insurance policy where the insured pays the premium, the benefits will not be subject to income tax. On a group disability policy where an employer pays the premium, the benefits are subject to income tax (except in those situations where the employee elects to pay with after-tax dollars, an option not always offered).

The following table may be helpful to you as a reference when filing claims with your carrier. It explains the different claim diagnosis categories your insurance company is likely to use.

CLAIM DIAGNOSIS CATEGORIES

CLAIM DIAGNOSIS CATEGORY	LAY LANGUAGE DESCRIPTION	SPECIFIC EXAMPLES
Diseases of the Musculoskeletal System & Connective Tissue	Muscle, Back & Joint Disorders	Arthritis, Herniated or Degenerated Disc, Back Pain, Spine/Joint Disorders, Cartilage Sprain, Tendonitis, Fibromyitis, Osteoporosis, Rheumatism, Scoliosis, Sciatica
Diseases of the Nervous System & Sense Organs	Spine & Nervous System Related Disorders	Multiple Sclerosis, Epilepsy, Paralysis, Alzheimer's, Parkinson's Disease, Amyotrophic Lateral Sclerosis (ALS), Bell's Palsy, Guillain-Barre Syndrome, Eye Disorders, including Diabetic Retinopathy & Macular Degeneration, Ear Disorders, including Balance Related Disorders like Menière's Disease
Diseases of the Circulatory System	Cardiovascular & Circulatory Diseases	Hypertension, Heart Disease, Heart Attack, Stroke, Aneurysm, Coronary Artery Disease, Phlebitis
Injury & Poisoning; Cancer & Neoplasms	Cancer & Tumors	Breast Cancer, Prostate Cancer, Lymphoma, Hodgkin's Disease, Leukemia, Tumors
Injuries &Accidents	Accidents, Injuries & Poisonings	Fractures, Sprains & Strains, Dislocations, Contusions, Burns, Poisoning, Allergic Reactions
Mental Disorders	Mental Illness & Behavioral Disorders	Depression, Schizophrenia, Drug/Alcohol/Substance Abuse, Bipolar Disorder, Anxiety, Obsessive-Compulsive Disorder
Diseases of the Respiratory System	Respiratory System Disorders	Influenza, Pneumonia, Asthma, Bronchitis, Emphysema, Pulmonary Fibrosis, Cystic Fibrosis, Chronic Obstructive Pulmonary Disorder (COPD)
Symptoms, Signs & Ill-Defined Conditions	Ill-Defined or Subjective Conditions	Headache, Insomnia, Coma, Chronic Fatigue Syndrome, Sleep Apnea, Seasonal Affective Disorder, Anorexia, other symptoms without a diagnosis
Infections & Parasitic Diseases	Infectious & Parasitic Diseases	Food Poisoning, HIV/AIDS, Hepatitis, Meningitis, Salmonella, Tuberculosis, Polio

CLAIM DIAGNOSIS CATEGORIES

CLAIM DIAGNOSIS CATEGORY	LAY LANGUAGE DESCRIPTION	SPECIFIC EXAMPLES
Diseases of the Digestive System	Digestive System Disorders	Gastric Ulcers, Gastritis, Appendicitis, Hernia, Irritable Bowel Syndrome, Cirrhosis of the Liver, Crohn's Disease, Diverticulitis, Ulcerative Colitis, Dental Disorders, Temporomandibular Joint Disorders (TMJ)
Endocrine, Nutritional & Metabolic Diseases & Immunity Disorders	Nutritional, Metabolic, Regulatory & Immunity Disorders	Diabetes, Malnutrition, Obesity, Gout, Cystic Fibrosis, Thyroid Disorders
Diseases of the Genitourinary System	Genital & Waste Removal Disorders	Uterine Prolapse, Cervicitis, Menopausal Symptoms, Kidney and Bladder Disorders, Genital Organ Disorders, Kidney Failure, Enlarged Prostate, Prostatitis, Urinary Tract Infections, Endometriosis
Complications of Pregnancy, Childbirth & the Puerperium	Pregnancy & Complications of Pregnancy	Normal Delivery, Caesarian Section, Complications of Pregnancy, Toxemia, Ectopic Pregnancy, Pre-Term Complications
Diseases of the Skin & Subcutaneous Tissue	Skin Conditions & Disorders	Eczema, Dermatitis, Cellulitis, Psoriasis, Sebaceous Cyst
Congenital Anomalies	Inherited Conditions	Congenital Anomalies, Spina Bifida, Down's Syndrome, Inherited Heart Valve Malfunction
Diseases of the Blood & Blood-Forming Organs	Blood-Related Disorders	Anemia, Hemophilia, Sickle-Cell Disease, Diseases of the Spleen
Other	Other Disorders	Other disorders not captured in categories above

Source: Council on Disability Awareness 2011 Long-Term Disability Claims Review

While we hope you never have to use your disability insurance, we also hope that you can feel secure in the knowledge that you have income protection in place if and when you need it.

CONCLUSION

Disability insurance is an exceedingly valuable component of financial planning. Disability insurance is also a very complex financial instrument and needs to be treated as such. Every day, disability insurance companies introduce new products and marketing concepts. As you've seen in this workbook, selecting and maintaining the "right" disability insurance policy and riders is a challenge.

While you shouldn't put off an important decision that would provide protection for your family, take the time to make sure you fully understand any policy you are considering. You should be comfortable with the company, agent, and product before purchasing anything.

The tools in this book were designed to assist you in understanding disability insurance and monitoring your portfolio more easily. Please keep in mind there is no substitute for the value that disability insurance can bring into play for providing the discounted dollars and income protection you need. Be sure the insurance agent gives you choices and options before you make a final decision.

After you have purchased an insurance policy, remember that you may have a "free-look" period—usually 10 to 30 days after you receive the policy—during which you can change your mind. Read your policy carefully during this time. If you decide not to keep it, the company will cancel the policy and provide an appropriate refund.

Review your policy periodically or when changes occur, such as changing occupations or employers or receiving an increase in earnings. An insurance agent can help you make sure your coverage is always aligned with your needs. Please see the last page of this workbook for information on keeping up to date through our websites and other online communications.

And remember, the more informed you are, the better the choices you can make.

APPENDIX

DISABILITY INSURANCE SOLUTIONS FOR YOUR BUSINESS

Business Overhead Expense (BOE)

BOE protects your regular monthly expenses that will allow your business to operate smoothly if you are unable to pay for your expenses due to a covered disability. It serves as a buoy to keep your daily operations afloat without interruption. Some examples of covered expenses include, but are not limited to, payroll for your employees, utility bills, employee benefits, taxes, office supplies, equipment leases, and your rent or mortgage at your office. Some policies even pay for the expense of hiring a replacement manager/executive who will be able to pick up where you left off.

Most businesses would sink if their day-to-day operations were in jeopardy. That's why it's best to go with the shortest waiting period possible in considering this plan. While you may have 3 months of savings to cover your personal expenses, it is often much more difficult to have enough money stashed away to keep your business afloat for more than a month while you are unable to work and not generating any new production.

Disability Insurance Buy/Sell Agreement (DIBS)

A DIBS policy will protect you in the same way a typical buy/sell policy would for life insurance, but in this case it's if your partner becomes disabled and can no longer pull her or his own weight. The policy would fund an agreement that mandates the purchase of the disabled partner's portion of the business. The DIBS benefit can be paid to you in an ongoing manner or as a lump sum.

Key Person Insurance

Key person insurance (sometimes referred to as key man insurance) is specifically designed to help your business if an important employee is no longer able to work due to a disabling illness or injury. Think about it: At least one person in your office is crucial to the daily success of your business. Maybe that person is you! This is a great tool to keep your business healthy and thriving if a valuable employee is no longer capable of selling your products; if your sound finances or operations are contingent upon the presence of your CFO or COO; or if your spokesperson or CEO can no longer be the figurehead he or she was hired to be. This policy will pay a benefit to your company so that your business does not suffer financially during your key person's absence.

ABBREVIATIONS AND ACRONYMS

AHIP—America's Health Insurance Plans

BOE—Business Overhead Expense

CFP—Certified Financial Planner

ChFC—Chartered Financial Consultants

CLU—Certified Life Underwriters

CPA-PF—Personal Financial Specialist

CPI—consumer price index

DIA—Disability Income Associate

DIBS—Disability Insurance Buy/Sell Agreement

ERISA—Employee Retirement Income Security Act of 1974

FSC—financial size category

IRIS—Insurance Regulatory Information Reports

LTD—Long-Term Disability Insurance

LUTCF—Life Underwriter Training Council Fellow

MIB—Medical Information Bureau

NAHU—National Association of Health Underwriters

NAIC—National Association of Insurance Commissioners

NAIFA—National Association of Insurance and Financial Advisors

PDQ—personal disability quotient

RBC—Risk Based Capital (system)

S&P—Standard & Poor's

SFSP—Society of Financial Services Professionals

SSA—Social Security Administration

SSDI—Social Security Disability Insurance

SSI—Supplemental Security Income

STD—Short-Term Disability Insurance

NOTES FROM THE AUTHORS

Dear Reader,

Disability insurance is simply a financial solution to a common problem—cash flow needs in the wake of a disabling illness or injury.

For better or for worse, there have been a wide array of products developed with differing language and mechanisms, all in the interest of customization and choice.

Unfortunately, those innumerable iterations can lead to a mounting sense of confusion, often resulting in inaction.

Your possession of this compressive DI resource already puts you ahead of the game.

The Q&A workbook was developed to help you distinguish what is important to your or your clients' needs by helping you organize what features are most necessary when structuring a DI plan.

We have been encouraged by positive reviews since the first edition of this book. We certainly hope it helps you accomplish your disability income goals, whatever they may be.

Sincerely,

Maxwell Schmitz, MSFS

Dear Reader,

Thank you for taking the time to learn all about disability insurance from the basic essentials to the finer points of disability insurance and how it fits into your financial life. I hope you are feeling more in control of your disability insurance and ready to implement your optimal disability insurance with *The Questions and Answers on Disability Insurance Workbook*.

If you loved the book and have a minute to spare, I would really appreciate a short review on your favorite book site. You're the reason why I continue to write about financial preparedness and advocate for integrity in financial services.

If you think this book might help a family member or friend with their own insurance, feel free to invite them to join the Get Ready Movement at www.tonysteuer.com. They'll receive the Get Ready Roadmap as well as helpful tips for reviewing all aspects of their money.

So what's next? Join the Get Ready Movement and stay up to date on the latest in changing the way we think about money by subscribing to the Get Ready! Newsletter and joining our community.

Thank you!

Tony

P.S. Listen to *The Get Ready Money Podcast*: Change the way you think about money. It includes insightful conversations with thought leaders that will provide you with practical advice that demystifies the complexities of finance and builds healthy habits that actually work.

P.S.S. If you are passionate about helping people feel empowered with their money, then please join the Get Ready! Expert Money Guides: Dedicated to Helping People Change the Way They Think about Money group on LinkedIn.

About the Authors

MAXWELL SCHMITZ, MSFS, is a third-generation expert in the disability insurance field. He studied Political Science and Psychology at the University of California, Davis, and received his Master of Science degree in Financial Services from the American College.

Max officially joined his family business at Yetworth Insurance Solutions (formerly DI & LTC Insurance Services), a disability and long-term care insurance general agency, in 2009. He has spent the beginning of his career specializing in the California disability insurance marketplace. At age 23, Max became a guest speaker at association meetings across the Bay Area. At 25, he became the President of the Marin County chapter of the National Association of Insurance and Financial Advisors. Following his term as President he became the Political Action Committee Chairman of NAIFA California. He currently sits on the NABIP LTC Working Group and is Vice President of the International DI Society.

Yetworth was pioneered as Bay Area Disability Insurance Services in the early 1980s, adding LTC to their repertoire in the early 1990s. Yetworth has a team that offers the most insightful service for these two very important, yet often misunderstood, lines of coverage.

The Yetworth difference is their personal touch and innovation as a client-facing wholesaler. They will guide advisors and their clients through the fact-finding process, all the way through policy delivery. Yetworth makes it simple for insurance agents and financial planners alike to learn and sell income protection products that will help your clients' families through the toughest of times.

TONY STEUER, CLU, LA, CPFFE, is an internationally recognized financial preparedness advocate, award-winning author, and podcaster. Known as a trailblazer in financial wellness, Tony's mission is to change the way we think about money.

Tony is the creator of the Get Ready Method, which is an easy-to-use roadmap to help you understand how everything fits together. It's based on eight habits that will empower you with money and transform your life. It includes an innovative and unique financial calendar system that provides a weekly action item to help you stay on track and keep all areas of your financial life up to date.

Tony is also an advisor at Paperwork and Dingo Technologies. He is a contributor to Forbes Advisor, as well as an expert content reviewer for NerdWallet. Tony is a member of Think Advisor's LUMINARIES class of 2022 as a finalist in Thought Leadership & Education. Tony served as a long-term member of the California Department of Insurance Curriculum Board.

Tony regularly consults with fintechs, financial planners, insurance agencies, attorneys, insurance companies, and other financial service companies on financial preparedness, insurance marketing, product best practices, and best practices. Tony is a past member of the National Financial Educator's Council (NFEC) Curriculum Advisory Board.

Tony is regularly featured in the media as an expert source, including ABC's *Seven on Your Side*, *Forbes*, NerdWallet, Cheddar TV, the *New York Times*, the *Washington Post*, *Fast Company*, the *Chicago Tribune*, CNBC, and Fox Business News. Tony is also a frequent guest on podcasts. Tony also served as a technical editor for The Retirement Bible and The Investing Bible.

He is passionate about giving back. Tony is involved with many worthwhile causes, including CLCS (Community Learning Center Schools—vice president) and JDRF (Juvenile Diabetes Research Foundation—volunteer), and has served on multiple boards and advisory committees. Tony has also been a coach for his son's basketball team and baseball teams, taught wilderness first aid and white-water rescue, volunteered as a white-water raft guide, and performed improvisational comedy.

Tony Steuer lives in Alameda, California.

Become a Get Ready Insider

The Get Ready Insider Program is a step-by-step system to help you get ready and stay prepared. It is based on eight habits that will empower you with your money and transform your life. The program includes an innovative and unique financial calendar system that provides the weekly action items (from this book) to help you stay on track and keep all areas of your financial life up to date.

The Get Ready Insider Program will help you

- learn healthy money habits to take control of your financial life,

- organize your financial life, and

- become fully empowered with your money so you can live the life you dream of.

As a Get Ready Insider, you'll receive access to the following:

- The Get Ready 52 weekly action item emails (Over 52 weeks, you'll receive a Weekly Accountability email with the action items from this book.)

- *The Get Ready! Blueprint* (fillable PDF version)

- The Get Ready Toolkit (100+ worksheets)

- Investment Policy Statement template

- Unclaimed property search worksheet

- Get Ready Movement Leader Kit: tools for clubs, masterminds, and teams

Learn more at www.tonysteuer.com.